Contemporary Issues in Mediation

Volume 8

Related Titles by the Singapore International Mediation Institute

---

Contemporary Issues in Mediation Volume 1
ISBN: 978-981-3108-35-6
ISBN: 978-981-3108-36-3 (pbk)

Contemporary Issues in Mediation Volume 2
ISBN: 978-981-3225-63-3
ISBN: 978-981-3225-64-0 (pbk)

Contemporary Issues in Mediation Volume 3
ISBN: 978-981-3270-81-7
ISBN: 978-981-3271-76-0 (pbk)

Contemporary Issues in Mediation Volume 4
ISBN: 978-981-120-911-6
ISBN: 978-981-120-928-4 (pbk)

Contemporary Issues in Mediation Volume 5
ISBN: 978-981-122-052-4
ISBN: 978-981-122-109-5 (pbk)

Contemporary Issues in Mediation Volume 6
ISBN: 978-981-124-142-0

Contemporary Issues in Mediation Volume 7
ISBN: 978-981-12-6871-7

Contemporary Issues in Mediation

Volume 8

Joel Lee
Singapore International Mediation Institute, Singapore &
National University of Singapore, Singapore

Marcus Lim
Lupl, Singapore

with Izzat Rashad Bin Rosazizi
National University of Singapore, Singapore

Guest Editor: Melvin Loh
Singapore University of Social Sciences, Singapore

SIMI SINGAPORE INTERNATIONAL MEDIATION INSTITUTE

World Scientific

Published by

World Scientific Publishing Co. Pte. Ltd.
5 Toh Tuck Link, Singapore 596224
USA office: 27 Warren Street, Suite 401-402, Hackensack, NJ 07601
UK office: 57 Shelton Street, Covent Garden, London WC2H 9HE

Library of Congress Cataloging-in-Publication Data
Names: Lee, Joel, editor. | Lim, Marcus, editor.
Title: Contemporary issues in mediation (v. 1) / Edited by Joel Lee
(Singapore International Mediation Institute, Singapore),
Marcus Lim (Singapore International Mediation Institute, Singapore).
Description: Hackensack, New Jersey : World Scientific, 2016.
Identifiers: LCCN 2016004240| ISBN 9789813108356 (hardcover : alk. paper) |
ISBN 9789813108363 (pbk.)
Subjects: LCSH: Dispute resolution (Law) | Mediation. | Dispute resolution (Law)--Singapore. | Mediation--Singapore.
Classification: LCC K2390 .C667 2016 | DDC 347/.09--dc23
LC record available at http://lccn.loc.gov/2016004240

Contemporary issues in mediation (v. 8)
ISBN 978-981-12-8524-0

British Library Cataloguing-in-Publication Data
A catalogue record for this book is available from the British Library.

For any available supplementary material, please visit
https://www.worldscientific.com/worldscibooks/10.1142/13649#t=suppl

Desk Editor: Claire Lum

Typeset by Stallion Press
Email: enquiries@stallionpress.com

What a wonderful opportunity for students of dispute resolution to be published in this excellent collection of essays! Several different essays examine commercial disputes including the implementation of the Singapore Convention — when countries refuse to enforce the convention or hesitations respectively in the EU and in China — as well as investor-state mediation; other essays dig into family and divorce mediation arguing for more inclusion, more flexibility and a broader approach to the emotional impact of these conflicts. And yet other essays question the actual structure of mediation — is it voluntary? And, in a very timely essay, how can we support the mediators themselves as they work to heal others? This is a terrific array of topics that is sure to provide useful information and thought-provoking reflections for its readers. Congratulations to SIMI for Volume 8.

Andrea Kupfer Schneider
Professor of Law, Cardozo School of Law
Director, Kukin Program for Conflict Resolution

The articles in it speak of a profession increasingly finding its own feet and self-confidence, as well as its place in the accepted societal and global order of dispute resolution. Speaking personally and as a (primarily) international commercial and investor/state mediator, I have learned much from other fields of mediation, and indeed from other disciplines beyond mediation. If I may offer one encouragement to all of us involved in mediation, it is to recognise the breadth of wisdom and learning across the whole mediation field — and beyond it — and to stay curious and open to what each of us can learn from others.

CIIM helps us to do just that. I recently had the pleasure and privilege of speaking at a private forum in Singapore for governments on the practicalities of investor-state mediation - it is no surprise that this kind of intellectual leadership arises from SIMI too. I am delighted to commend this edition to you.

Bill Marsh
International Mediator
SIMI Certified Mediator

https://doi.org/10.1142/9789811285257_fmatter

Contents

https://doi.org/10.1142/9789811285257_fmatter

Foreword for the Series

William Ury

A young man was hiking through the woods. He came to a clearing and sat on a rock to rest. As he ate his lunch, he noticed an old man moving through the clearing in a very deliberate way. The man would walk a specific number of steps, poke a hole in the ground with his walking stick, drop something in and then repeat the process. Curious, the young man approached the old man and asked him what he was doing.

> *The old man replied, "Well, I'm planting trees."*
> *"But why?" the young man asked.*
> *"When I was younger," the old man said, "this entire land was filled with trees. But over time, many trees had been cut down. I come here every day to plant trees."*
> *Fascinated, the young man asked, "How long have you been doing this?"*
> *"Forty years." was the matter of fact reply.*
> *"Forty years!" exclaimed the young man.*
> *"Yup," the old man replied. Gesturing to a grove of young trees in the distance, he said with some pride, "I planted those 10 years ago."*
> *The young man was incredulous. "That's great but these trees will take a long time to grow! And, if you will pardon me saying so, you may not live long enough to see the seeds you are planting today grow into trees!"*
> *"This is true," said the old man "I have lived long enough to see some of the fruits of my labour. But the seeds I plant today are not for me, but for you."*

It has now been just about 40 years since I had the privilege of embarking on the adventure of teaching and practicing in the field of negotiation and mediation. During that time, I have had the joy of learning from and working with many highly talented and skilled individuals in academia, law, business and diplomacy. In those early days, there was very little scholarly writing in this area. After all, the field was relatively new and viewed by many with caution, if not outright skepticism.

Over the years, I have been gratified to watch the field of mediation grow considerably. Today, practitioners, teachers and researchers can be found in every part of the world. The teaching, practice and scholarship of negotiation and mediation constitute a dynamic system in which each contributes to the others. New tools and frameworks have been developed as a result of research, taught to practitioners, and then tested and refined in the field, which in turn has informed further research. This interplay between theory and practice has been vital in developing new insights and methods.

Yet the field of negotiation and mediation is still young. As we look back on the progress, we might be satisfied with the seeds we have planted which have sprouted into trees. Yet, as the concepts and practices spread around the world, we have a responsibility to ensure that future generations will be able to build on all that has been achieved. We must continue to plant seeds, not for ourselves, but for those to come.

This is why this book project by the Singapore International Mediation Institute is such a timely endeavour worthy of support. It is said that a journey of a thousand miles begins with a single step. The Singapore International Mediation Institute is taking that first step to inspire the youth of today and encourage them to engage in scholarship about mediation. It provides them the platform and the opportunity to plant seeds for the benefit and enjoyment of future generations.

As the first of its kind in Singapore, I look forward to seeing this book series not only continue to flourish, but also to show the way forward through innovative and thought-provoking work.

And I take this opportunity to wish you much success in getting to yes!

William Ury
Co-founder, Harvard Negotiation Project
Co-author, *Getting to Yes*
31 May 2016

https://doi.org/10.1142/9789811285257_fmatter

About the Guest Editor

Melvin Loh is a Senior Lecturer with the School of Law, Singapore University of Social Sciences. A graduate of the Faculty of Law, National University of Singapore as well as the Singapore Management University Yong Pung How School of Law, he specialises in mediation and negotiation, as well as criminal law. He has also undergone extensive training in the field of appropriate dispute resolution, most recently at the Program on Negotiation at Harvard Law School. In 2023, he was awarded the SUSS Excellence in Teaching Award.

Melvin is a Certified Mediator with the Singapore International Mediation Institute and an empaneled Associate Mediator and trainer with the Singapore Mediation Centre. With over a decade of experience in mediation, he has mediated a vast spectrum of cases both inside and outside the Courts, including criminal, family, commercial, and real estate, among others. He has also taught, trained, and assessed in multiple international jurisdictions in furtherance of the development of mediation.

An active volunteer at heart, Melvin assists as an advocate and solicitor with various pro bono initiatives of the Law Society of Singapore, which include the Criminal Legal Aid Scheme ("CLAS"), Community Legal Clinics ("CLC") and Legal Aid Bureau matters. Melvin also provides representation in matters through the Legal Assistance Scheme for Capital Offences ("LASCO").

He serves as an Executive Committee member with the Mediation Committee of the Law Society of Singapore, as well as the CLAS and the CLC Committees of Pro Bono SG.

Melvin is also a lifelong volunteer outside of his legal profession, giving time to help with various causes such as with at-risk families, youth, and foreign workers.

https://doi.org/10.1142/9789811285257_fmatter

About the Editors

Joel Lee is a Professor at the Faculty of Law, National University of Singapore. Joel co-pioneered the teaching of Negotiation and Mediation in the Singapore universities and has played a significant role in furthering the development of mediation in Singapore, not just in education but in practice. A graduate of Victoria University of Wellington and Harvard Law School, Joel is a partner with CMP Cambridge (USA) and a principal mediator with the Singapore Mediation Centre.

Joel was a member of the International Mediation Institute's Independent Standards Commission and Intercultural Taskforce and was also a key member of the Ministry of Law's Working Group on International Commercial Mediation. Joel is presently the founding Chair of the Board of the Singapore International Mediation Institute. He is also a Certified Trainer of Neuro-Linguistic Programming (NLP).

Joel has taught overseas at the University of Copenhagen (Denmark); University of Law, Economics and Science of Aix-Marseille (Aix-en-Provence France); and Anglia Law School (UK) and is the co-editor and co-author of the book *An Asian Perspective on Mediation* and the *Singapore Mediation Handbook*, and the General Editor for the *Asian Journal on Mediation*. In 2011, Joel was awarded the Outstanding Educator Award, which is the National University of Singapore's highest teaching award.

Marcus Lim is the Country Manager (Singapore) for Lupl. Lupl is the open industry platform for legal matters that brings together in one place the people, conversations, documents, data and knowledge for legal matters, providing real-time 360-degree visibility and control.

Prior to joining Lupl, Marcus was the first Executive Director, and later CEO, of the Singapore International Mediation Institute (SIMI), where he spearheaded many initiatives in growing the organisation into an internationally recognised and credible brand for mediation standards.

He holds appointments as Adjunct Assistant Professor for Negotiation and Mediation Workshops at the Faculty of Law, National University of Singapore, and was the coordinator for both courses in 2017. A graduate from the prestigious Law and Business Double Degree programme at the National University of Singapore, he is a consultant with CMP Cambridge (USA). He is certified in the Thomas-Kilmann Instrument for Conflict and Change Management. Marcus is a SIMI Certified Mediator, an Associate Mediator with the Singapore Mediation Centre and a court-appointed volunteer mediator for the Small Claims Tribunal at the State Courts. Prior to joining SIMI, Marcus practiced at Rajah & Tann LLP's Competition and Technology, Media and Telecommunications Practice Group.

Marcus has extensive experience conducting negotiation and mediation trainings for staff and in the management of government organisations, as well as multinational corporations across a diverse range of sectors, such as finance, retail, real estate, IT, education and the healthcare industry.

https://doi.org/10.1142/9789811285257_fmatter

Editors' Note

It has been three years since the ratification of the Singapore Convention on Mediation ("SCM"). The SCM has arguably created a profound impact on thought leadership in the area of mediation and has since engendered rich discourse on its applicability and feasibility in the world of modern mediation practice. These developments highlight and underscore the SCM's increasing importance in the ongoing effort to recognise mediation globally as a legitimate and effective means of dispute resolution.

Volume 8 constitutes the latest edition to the Contemporary Issues in Mediation series and adds further food for thought to this rich discourse with nine thought-provoking essays that shed light on the diversity of issues and challenges that define the contemporary mediation landscape today.

The SCM is one of the central topics discussed in this Volume. The top entry, "Operationalising Article 5(1)(e) of the Singapore Convention on Mediation" by Valerie Lim, scrutinises the definition and required threshold of certain terms used in the aforementioned Article in the SCM, and discusses whether evidentiary proof requirements may affect the confidentiality of the mediation process. Other essays on this topic highlight certain challenges of the SCM from a more macro perspective, such as the reasons behind the hesitation in adopting the SCM in both the European Union (Elyssa Tan, runner-up entry) and China (Tao Chongyang).

Another central topic examined by this Volume is the multitude of issues surrounding mediation in the context of family disputes. The essays in this Volume discuss, *inter alia*, the unique role of a family mediator in dealing with "high conflict personalities" (Neo Xin Xuan), the interrelatedness of mediation, therapeutic justice and the family justice system in Singapore (Christabelle Tan), and whether it would be in the "best interest" of children to be involved in divorce mediation processes (Tan Pei Han).

Aside from these two central topics, the other essays in this volume also provide meaningful discussions on mediator burnout (Gini Wong), the potentially oxymoronic nature of mandatory mediation (Nicole Ng) and the tension between confidentiality and transparency in investor-State mediation processes (Fan Xiaoyu).

As always, this publication would not have been possible without the support and effort of many people. We would like to take this opportunity to express our heartfelt thanks to:

- Our wonderful families, for their unending patience and love;
- Mr Izzat Rashad Bin Rosazizi, for his dedicated and invaluable professional assistance to the editorial team;
- Mr William Ury, for writing the foreword for the series;
- Members of SIMI's board, past and present for their unwavering support of the project (Mr Calvin Phua, Professor Nadja Alexander, Mr Poon Hong Yuen, Mr Han Kok Juan, Ms Josephine Hadikusumo, Mr Michael Leathes and Ms Irena Vanenkova);
- The Singapore Ministry of Law, for continuing to support our work;
- The National University of Singapore Faculty of Law, for being a stalwart supporter of SIMI's operations;
- Our publishers, the World Scientific Publishing Company for their patience and guidance in bringing another volume to publication; and
- Our students (past and present) from the National University of Singapore Faculty of Law, the Singapore Management University Yong Pung How School of Law, the Singapore University of Social Sciences School of Law, as well as all over the world, for always being an inspiration to our work.

Last but not least, we would like to thank you, the reader, for supporting SIMI and this book. We hope that this project continues to inspire you in your work, whatever field it may be, to find collaborative solutions in resolving your disputes.

Joel Lee, Marcus Lim and Melvin Loh
Singapore
21 September 2023

https://doi.org/10.1142/9789811285257_fmatter

About the CIIM Essay Competition

As part of SIMI's (Singapore International Mediation Institute) mission to promote awareness and interest in mediation, SIMI regularly organises an essay competition to help promote mediation academia among undergraduates and students in tertiary institutions. Submissions are welcome from students not only pursuing studies in law but also other disciplines. Selected entries will be featured in an annual edition of the *Contemporary Issues in Mediation*, with attractive prizes for some of the best submissions.

About SIMI

The Singapore International Mediation Institute (SIMI) was incorporated on 15 July 2014 as a non-profit organisation supported by the Ministry of Law. SIMI is a subsidiary of the National University of Singapore (NUS) and is housed at the NUS Faculty of Law.

SIMI is headed by an international Board of Directors with representatives from both mediation practitioners as well as corporate users of mediation, to further its mission to (1) set and achieve high mediation standards through the professionalisation of mediation; (2) promote understanding and inspire the use of mediation; (3) stimulate and facilitate the development and growth of mediation through research and innovation; and (4) foster a strong mediation community in Asia by engaging stakeholders in discussion, events and outreach activities.

https://doi.org/10.1142/9789811285257_0001

Operationalising Article 5(1)(e) of the Singapore Convention on Mediation

Valerie Lim An Qi

Drawing on the 1958 New York Convention[1] in international arbitration for inspiration, the 2019 Singapore Convention on Mediation ("SCM")[2] provides for the enforcement of settlement agreements in international commercial disputes. To date, the SCM has 56 signatories, of which 11 are parties to the New York Convention.[3] This paper explores Article 5(1)(e) of the SCM ("Grounds for refusing to grant relief"), which reads:

> "The competent authority of the Party to the Convention where relief is sought under article 4 may refuse to grant relief at the request of the party against whom the relief is sought only if that party furnishes to the competent authority proof that:
>
> (e) There was a serious breach by the mediator of standards applicable to the mediator or the mediation without which breach that party would not have entered into the settlement agreement;"

I. Preliminary discussion of Article 5(1)(e)

Some preliminary points may be observed from the recital to Article 5(1). Firstly, refusal of relief remains discretionary ("may"). The *Handbook on the SCM*[4] confirms that the Article 5 grounds are "permissive", which means that the enforcing authority may still grant relief even if it finds that one of the grounds under Article 5 is present. Secondly, an application for the refusal of relief under Article 5(1) must be made at the request "of the party against whom the relief is sought". In other words, the enforcing party cannot consider the ground on its own initiative, in contrast to the grounds under Article 5(2). This closely resembles the regime under the New York Convention for international arbitration.[5] Thirdly, the party seeking to challenge enforcement must "furnish to the competent authority proof" that the ground(s) under Article 5(1) are satisfied.

Additionally, it appears from a plain textual reading of Article 5(1)(e) that the "serious breach" of standards must have been committed "by the mediator". However, given that the SCM applies to international commercial mediation where the majority of parties are typically represented by lawyers,[6] this raises an open question: what happens if there is a serious breach of the applicable standards committed by a mediation advocate for the party? One possibility could be to ask whether such misconduct can be attributed to the mediator, for instance because of the latter's failure to intervene. Another possibility could be to resist enforcement on some other ground instead, for instance Article 5(1)(a) (party incapacity).

II. The requirements of a "serious" and operative breach

Pursuant to Article 5(1)(e), there must have been a "serious breach", "without which breach that party would not have entered into the settlement agreement". Conceivably, one way of measuring the "seriousness" of a breach is by reference to its effect on the parties. Nonetheless, Kallipetis (who was present at the Working Group II discussions) argues that these two requirements are *cumulative*.[7]

A. *Objective assessment of "seriousness"*

It can be observed from the drafting history of the SCM that the word "serious" was added "to introduce an objective assessment of the alleged breach in order to avoid claims that are fanciful, immaterial, and subjective".[8] Terms such as "gross misconduct", "violate", "material impact", "undue influence", "manifest failure" and "fair treatment" had previously been proposed but were ultimately rejected by the drafters.[9] This was because such terms were deemed "ambiguous, unknown in certain legal traditions and might introduce uncertainties".[10] The drafting history thus confirms the intention of the drafters, i.e., the intention "to incorporate more objective standards with a higher threshold"[11] under Article 5(1)(e).

However, without illustrations, it remains unclear what exactly would amount to a "serious" breach of mediator or mediation standards. To put it another way: what would cross the "higher threshold" of more objective standards?

B. *"Without which breach that party would not have entered into the settlement agreement"*

The intention behind this element can be elucidated from the drafting history of Article 5(1)(e). One suggestion was to combine what are now Articles 5(1)(e) and (1)(f) to read: "a material breach of applicable standards by the conciliator but for which a reasonable party would not have entered into a settlement agreement".[12] The *travaux preparatoires* explains that the "but for" phrase was intended to "ensure that the ground could be invoked only when the consent of the parties to enter into a settlement agreement had been vitiated".[13]

This accords with the fundamental principle of party self-determination in mediation. In the SMC itself, "mediation" is defined as a process involving, *inter alia*, the assistance of a third person (the mediator) who "lack[s] the authority to impose a solution upon the parties to the dispute".[14] The *Model Standards of Conduct for Mediators* (2005), which was developed by three leading American organisations in the field of mediation and has since proved to be an influential ethical source for mediators, mediation scholars and legislatures,[15] likewise recognises the "fundamental principle" that:

> "A mediator shall conduct a mediation based on the principle of party self-determination. *Self-determination is the act of coming to a voluntary, uncoerced decision in which each party makes free and informed choices as to process and outcome...*"[16] [emphasis added]

Accordingly, this explains the fundamental difference between mediation and arbitration. Since an arbitrator decides the issues between the parties, it was thought that there is a real risk of bias and improper behaviour affecting the arbitrator's decision to the detriment of one party.[17] On the other hand, since a mediator lacks any authority to impose a solution upon the parties, mediator misconduct was reasoned to "only be relevant if it vitiates a party's consent to a settlement".[18] Furthermore, it must be borne in mind that parties in international commercial disputes are typically represented by lawyers, whose role includes "to protect [parties'] interests, guide their decisions, and ensure that their consent to the settlement [is] informed and genuine".[19]

C. *Proving vitiation of consent*

In this regard, the burden of proving the causal link (i.e., that the relevant breach vitiated a party's consent in entering into the settlement agreement) is on the party seeking to set it aside. However, the standard of proof may differ across jurisdictions, depending on the prevailing judicial attitude towards mediation and the policy of supporting mediated settlements. For instance, under US case law, the courts are eager to enforce settlements and have established a strong presumption that a settlement reflects the exercise of parties' self-determination, and generally require a strong showing to overcome this presumption.[20] It has been observed that many such complaints concerning mediator impropriety were unsuccessful because the US courts "assume[d] that parties are sufficiently protected when they are legally represented".[21] At the Working Group II meetings, experienced mediators similarly warned against pandering to "Settlors Remorse".[22]

On the one hand, taking independent legal advice into account as a significant factor promotes the policy of supporting mediated settlements, which the courts have especially articulated in respect of commercial transactions.[23] On the other hand, however, those who prefer a "richer version of [protecting] party self-determination" may argue that the burden of proof can be modified. Drawing inspiration from Welsh's proposal in the coercion context,[24] firstly, the party alleging misconduct needs to show a "probable cause standard". In this regard, the party's subjective feeling that their consent was vitiated, coupled with evidence of the mediator's misconduct, might be able to meet this standard.[25] If the court finds probable cause, the evidential burden then shifts to the mediator, to prove that the party's agreement was free and voluntary (i.e., that their consent was not vitiated).

Nonetheless, Welsh also goes on to recognise that this modification of the burden of proof could "have several very unfortunate consequences".[26] Reducing the evidential burden on the complaining party could disincentivise people from serving as mediators if they realise that they may be forced to prove that there was no operative mediator misconduct. Furthermore, mediation itself could become the source of much litigation, and confidentiality would be compromised under these circumstances.[27] Thus, it is submitted that the preferable approach is to strike a balance between (i) promoting finality of mediated settlements, and (ii) preventing the abuse of parties' self-determination where appropriate.

III. The question of evidential proof (and its relationship with mediation confidentiality)

Next, there is the question of evidential proof (i.e. that the party resisting enforcement has to prove each element of Article 5(1)(e)) and how it affects mediation confidentiality.

From the *travaux preparatoires*, the Report of the Working Group II (Dispute Settlement) explained that Article 5(1)(e) was not intended to "impact the confidential nature of conciliation and that the enforcing authority would generally not be expected to inquire into the details of the process".[28] However, it is submitted that this may be more apparent than real. Depending on the particular standard at issue, judicial oversight necessarily involves the courts inquiring into the relevant details of the mediation process, and sometimes the relevant parts of the subject matter(s) of the mediation. For instance, in deciding whether an alleged settlement agreement was binding in *Surindar Singh s/o Jaswant Singh v Sita Jaswant Kaur*,[29] the Singapore Court of Appeal scrutinised the parties' correspondence post-mediation and reproduced paragraphs which recounted mediation communications (although Quek Anderson observes that it is arguable that the parties may have waived their privilege in that case).[30]

Furthermore, due to the varying approaches between the common law and civil law jurisdictions to mediation confidentiality, the ability to prove claims under Article 5(1)(e) will vary across jurisdictions.[31]

Even the common law jurisdictions do not share a unified approach, with Kallipetis observing that there seems to be two broad camps. On the one hand, some jurisdictions consider mediation to be "no more than assisted 'without prejudice' negotiations". On the other hand, others consider that mediation has an "entirely separate privilege of its own", either regarding mediation privilege as absolute or recognising that the privilege may permit the admission of evidence "in the interests of justice".[32]

A. *Recognising categorical exceptions to mediation confidentiality/privilege*

The trend of both UK and Singapore case law appears to regard mediation confidentiality as akin to assisted "without prejudice" negotiations, and subject it to the various categorical exceptions. In Singapore, Section 9 of the Mediation Act 2017 (2020 Rev Ed) lists the various exceptions to the general rule against disclosure of mediation communication. Of particular relevance to Article 5(1)(e) SCM is that where leave of court is obtained, mediation communication may be disclosed "for the purpose of enforcing or disputing a mediated settlement agreement".[33]

Under the UK common law, "without prejudice" privilege can be waived by the parties or when the circumstances of the case fit the limited exceptions set out in *Unilever Plc v The Procter & Gamble Co.*[34] At present, the courts have not yet reviewed all the exceptions in connection to mediation,[35] but one that may be potentially relevant to the SCM is the recognition in *Unilever* (at [23]) that:

> "Apart from any concluded contract or estoppel, one party may be allowed to give evidence of what the other said or wrote without prejudice negotiations *if the exclusion of the evidence would act as a cloak for perjury, blackmail or other 'unambiguous impropriety'*".[36]
>
> [emphasis added]

However, this does not align perfectly with Article 5(1)(e) SCM as it appears that the standard for "ambiguous impropriety" is high and the English courts would only apply the exception "in exceptional circumstances" which "show the clearest abuse of privilege",[37] such as alleged blackmail.[38] At present, it is unclear whether this high standard for "unambiguous impropriety" under UK common law coincides with the standard of a "serious breach" under Article 5(1)(e).

A further complication is that most of the UK case law (in the mediation context and otherwise) concerning the "unambiguous conduct" exception deals with allegations of such (mis)conduct by parties. For instance, in *Farm Assist Ltd v Secretary of State for the Environment, Food and Rural Affairs (DEFRA) (No. 2)*,[39] the alleged "illegitimate pressure" concerned DEFRA's conduct at mediation and the contents of its mediation statement,[40] and whether this amounted to economic duress. Similarly, academic discussion has traditionally focused on the standard for "impropriety" in relation to a party's conduct, for instance arguing that adopting an adversarial position or using hard bargaining tactics in mediation alone are unlikely to qualify as "unambiguous impropriety".[41] Thus, it may be difficult to transpose current jurisprudence on the "unambiguous impropriety" exception in *Unilever* to the context of Article 5(1)(e) SCM, which deals with the *mediator's* misconduct.

While such an approach of setting out categorical exceptions to mediation confidentiality/privilege is laudable for its certainty, it has been pointed out that it could also create "incentives that are inconsistent with the goals of mediation".[42] In particular, allowing an exception to mediation confidentiality whenever mediator misconduct is raised would "effectively [wipe] out any assurance of confidentiality whenever a purported mediated agreement is litigated".[43] This coheres with the discussions of the Working Group II, where experienced mediators warned against pandering to "Settlors Remorse".[44]

B. *The balancing approach*

In contrast, the US Uniform Mediation Act ("UMA") provides an interesting alternative to the question of mediation confidentiality that promotes flexibility. Where there are court proceedings to advance a defence to avoid liability under "a contract arising out of the mediation", the UMA prescribes a balancing test of whether the "need for the evidence ... substantially outweighs the interest in protecting confidentiality".[45] Furthermore, this determination is to be made in a hearing *in camera.*[46]

It is submitted that such a balancing test is preferable, since it is "customised to the circumstances of each case" and "a more nuanced way"[47] to take into account both the seriousness of the misconduct claim and the invasiveness of the threat to mediation confidentiality. Ultimately, there is a real need for the enforcement of mediated agreements "to be decided within a framework that recognises mediation's unique character"[48] — and mediation confidentiality is one defining reason why parties are increasingly attracted to mediation.

Hence, it is hoped that the courts may be sensitive to preserving mediation confidentiality. Even if a categorical approach is adopted, practical measures such as (i) anonymising parties' names,[49] (ii) anonymising certain parts of the reproduced mediation communications[50] (in particular those which are closely connected to the subject matter of the mediation),[51] as well as (iii) holding *in camera* hearings for the determination of admissibility of mediation communications may help to preserve mediation confidentiality. For instance, in Singapore, Quek Anderson suggests that further inspiration can also be taken from the practical guidance provided to the courts when reviewing arbitration awards under the Arbitration Act 2001 and International Arbitration Act 1994.[52]

IV. "Standards applicable to the mediator or the mediation" and the question of *whose* standards

At the outset, there is no strict definition of the 'standards' referred to by Article 5(1)(e) SCM, but the *travaux preparatoires* recognises that standards could take "different forms" such as national law and codes of conduct, including those developed by professional associations.[53]

A. *The problem with a diversity of standards*

Nonetheless, there remains the open question of *whose* standards are "applicable" under Article 5(1)(e) SCM. The clearest instance may be when mediators engaging in international commercial mediation subscribe to a Code of Conduct or a Code of Ethics which is expressly identified in the mediation agreement.[54] Apart from this, the *travaux preparatoires* also recognises the possibility of standards (i) applicable at the place where the mediation took place, or (ii) the place where enforcement was sought.[55] Whether one or more standards can be "applicable to the mediator or mediation" under Article 5(1)(e), or whether Article 5(1)(e) would require the enforcing authority to consider the most appropriate standard, remains an open question.

If the former position is taken, then the problem of conflicting standards may arise. For instance, mediator "impartiality" is not a universal mediator characteristic in practice.[56] Standard II of the Model Standards of Conduct for Mediators defines "impartiality" as "freedom from favouritism, bias or prejudice", and requires mediators to "avoid conduct that gives the appearance of partiality".[57] Standard 4.1 of the Singapore International Mediation Institute (SIMI) Code of Professional Conduct for SIMI Mediators provides that its mediators should act in an "independent, neutral and impartial way" and "treat all relevant parties to the mediation with fairness, equality and respect".[58] In contrast, in many non-Western cultures, mediators are not "disinterested" outsiders to the dispute, but are sought out precisely because they know the parties and are already aware of the dispute.[59]

If the latter position is taken (i.e., that only one set of "standards" are applicable), then the question is how to determine the most appropriate standard. Much like how the subject of choice of law has evolved to assess what law should be applied to determine the outcome of substantive disputes involving cross-border elements, there may be a need to develop a mechanism by which enforcing authorities in state parties to the SCM can determine whose standards to apply in a way which produces consistent outcomes. While it is conceivable that the enforcing state may wish to apply its own standards (in the absence of an express choice in the mediation agreement), doing so may not always protect parties' reasonable expectations or respect international comity. Ultimately, there is also a need to articulate the normative theory underpinning Article 5(1)(e) SCM — i.e., whether it serves only to protect the reasonable expectations as between parties, or whether broader public interests (such as a mediator's duty to the profession of mediation and the public)[60] may also be at play.

B. *Further need for harmonisation*

As such, there is a need for further harmonisation — if not of uniform standards for mediators in international commercial disputes, then at least of a mechanism by which the appropriate standards may be determined. Currently, there are discussions to try and establish a uniform Code of Conduct for mediators.[61] A plurality of standards, whilst giving effect to the flexibility that mediation offers, also raises concerns that Article 5(1)(e) "could open doors for the enforcing authority to refuse enforcement based on diverse grounds, which would [instead] run contrary to the flexible nature of [mediation]".[62]

V. Conclusion

Some delegates at the Working Group II meetings thought that there was "no need" to provide the familiar safeguards (borrowed from the arbitration context) for protecting a party in the mediation context, given that mediators lack the authority to impose a solution upon the parties.[63] Furthermore, empirical evidence from the US shows that the misconduct ground of challenge is traditionally under-utilised.[64] However, it is submitted that this overlooks the importance of *process fairness* as between the parties, and Article 5(1)(e) SCM is a welcome step towards upholding this. The challenge remains for Article 5(1)(e) to be operationalised within a framework that recognises mediation's unique character,[65] and for the ambiguities concerning its various elements — for instance, the current diversity of standards, questions of evidential proof and confidentiality, and the threshold standard of "seriousness" — to be further clarified by the international community and/or the courts of enforcing states.

https://doi.org/10.1142/9789811285257_0002

The Hesitation of the European Union in Adopting the Singapore Convention on Mediation: Perspectives from International Relations Theory

Elyssa Tan

I. Introduction

On 7 August 2019, the United Nations Convention on International Settlement Agreements Resulting from Mediation (the "Singapore Convention") was made open for signature after several years of development by the United Nations Commission on International Trade Law. The Singapore Convention is the first international instrument to provide a global legal framework for the enforcement of mediated settlement agreements ("MSA") resulting from cross-border commercial disputes, and has been signed by 56 states and ratified by 10 at the time of writing.[1]

In recent years, the worldwide increase in cross-border transactions and trade has naturally seen a proportional increase in the instances of commercial disputes arising between private parties in different states. In the face of high legal costs and prolonged court processes involved in cross-border litigation, mediation has risen in popularity as a cost-effective and efficient alternative means of resolving disputes amicably.

Nevertheless, a secondary challenge arises where, following a successful mediation, a MSA is signed but one of the parties breaches its terms by, for instance, failing to perform an agreed-upon obligation, or refusing to pay a settlement sum. In such cases, the aggrieved party would then have to return to a court to enforce the terms of the MSA by commencing a fresh legal suit against the non-complying party to seek a court order for the appropriate relief against the latter. The aggrieved party would then have to bear the costly and time-consuming burden of court processes again — which could well be in a foreign court — and the prospect of this would essentially undermine the fundamental benefits of mediation[2] and discourage parties from attempting mediation in the first place.

The Singapore Convention ostensibly provides a solution to this conundrum by establishing a harmonised global legal framework for the seamless enforcement of MSAs resulting from cross-border commercial disputes. Under this streamlined framework, all an aggrieved party needs to do when an MSA is breached is to submit the MSA to a court of a signatory state to the Singapore Convention, which will be able to grant the appropriate relief automatically. This landmark development in international law ultimately aims to promote the use of mediation in amicably settling international commercial disputes, which would, in turn, "contribute to the development of harmonious international relations".[3]

II. Why the hesitation of the European Union ("EU") in adopting the Singapore Convention?

Given the inextricable link between international politics and global trade, the Singapore Convention has the potential to substantially benefit the international political arena should more states sign on, as relations between major commercial entities in different states would be lubricated via the universal framework. Notwithstanding this, it is puzzling that the EU and all its member states have yet to put pen to paper on the Singapore Convention and have even expressed hesitation in doing so.[4]

Several rather unilluminating reasons have been cited for this reticence. First, it has been stated that the EU is still deliberating whether to sign on to the Singapore Convention as a regional economic entity, or whether its individual member states should do so separately.[5] However, neither the details of such discussions nor the reasons behind why they are necessary has been publicised to-date.

Next, it has been suggested that the development of the EU's own legal instrument pertaining to cross-border mediation — the Directive 2008/52/EC on Certain Aspects of Mediation in Civil and Commercial Matters (the "EU Mediation Directive") — should be prioritised.[6] This is purportedly because the EU Mediation Directive establishes similar guidelines pertaining to cross-border enforcement of private agreements,[7] and shares a similar purpose with the Singapore Convention of "[promoting] further the use of mediation and [ensuring] that [EU member states] can rely on a predictable legal framework".[8] Yet, the presence of this overlap does not mean that the Singapore Convention cannot co-exist with the EU Mediation Directive, and no further explanation has been publicly provided as to why this preference should, in theory, be held.

Finally, there has been concern expressed that the enforcement mechanisms under the Singapore Convention may render superfluous or contradict well-entrenched domestic legal principles in the individual member states.[9] It is curious that this concern has even been raised, as EU member states are obliged to mirror in their domestic laws the provisions of the EU Mediation Directive — which are not inconsistent with the Singapore Convention.[10] In any event, it is not inconceivable for appropriate amendments to be made to domestic laws to bring them in line with the Singapore Convention. It remains to be seen why the EU member states appear to perceive the seemingly minor drawback of doing so as outweighing the potential international benefits of the Singapore Convention.

Given the palpable lacunas in these reasons and the potentially political nature of the issue at hand, it would be illuminating to complete the picture by venturing a further analysis of the issue using international relations ("IR") theory. This essay will attempt to elucidate a theoretical basis for the EU member states' hesitation in adopting the Singapore Convention by exploring the foregoing three reasons from three different IR perspectives in the hopes of shedding further light on this state of affairs.

III. Theoretical perspectives

A. *Liberal institutionalism*

When regarding a well-established institution such as the EU, it is apposite to begin our analysis with an "institutional approach"[11] to explore the impact, if any, of this institution on the actions of its member states. Accordingly, the rationalist theory of Liberal Institutionalism will first be relied on to dig deeper into the motivations behind the individual EU member states in hesitating to adopt the Singapore Convention.

The Liberal Institutionalist perspective in IR theory begins with the assumption that the international system is anarchic in nature, but that such anarchy may be attenuated by the presence of international institutions. These institutions act as a vehicle through which cooperation between states is promoted, as they aid competitive states in discovering commonalities in their interests and maximising their "absolute gains" through formal collaborative arrangements.[12]

From a state's perspective, such an institution essentially imposes constraints on their behaviour and choices available to them to pursue their interests.[13] Put otherwise, decisions taken by these individual states adhere to a "logic of expected consequences", where states pursue their interests only within the confines of the values represented by the institution and "choose among alternatives by evaluating their likely consequences for personal or collective objectives, conscious that other actors are doing likewise".[14]

The EU is, doubtless, an institution falling within the definition propounded in Liberal Institutionalism. Birthed from the benevolent belief that "conflict between states could be reduced by creating a common interest in trade and economic collaboration",[15] the EU has held itself out as an institution promoting cooperation and coherence among states located in the European geographical region in respect of policy areas such as the economy, health, trade, and human rights, with the ultimate goal of "peace, stability and prosperity".[16]

With this backdrop in mind, it is unsurprising that the behaviour of EU member states has been characterised by hesitation when presented with a legal framework which is, on its face, extraneous to the EU. Applying the tenets of Liberal Institutionalism, the presence of the EU ipso facto constrains the decisions that member states would otherwise take vis-à-vis the Singapore Convention in the pursuit of their interests. Accordingly, if a member state were to consider the merits of the Singapore Convention, it is compelled to deliberate between the likely consequences of (a) adopting the Singapore Convention unilaterally for its personal objectives, and (b) refraining from doing so and pursuing the collective objectives flowing from prioritising the subsisting legal order in the union — all while being conscious that other member states may be doing the same. This is a conceivable theoretical basis for why the discussions as to whether the Singapore Convention should be signed by the EU collectively or as individual member states are even necessary in the first place.

Exacerbating these deliberations is also the EU Mediation Directive, which not only serves as a "formal collaborative arrangement"[17] birthed from the institution but also lays down mandatory guidelines which EU member states are obliged to implement in their domestic laws.[18] The very presence of this formal arrangement as a product of the overseeing institution is likely to be an element operating in EU member states' deliberations, and they would understandably be hesitant to subordinate this subsisting legal order representing the collective objectives of the union, to the global instrument of the Singapore Convention. Furthermore, the "seemingly minor drawback" of amending domestic laws to bring them in line with the Singapore Convention may have the converse effect of jeopardising the "absolute gains" the institution seeks to enhance through the guidelines in the EU Mediation Directive. This would conceivably be a major downside, as compared to the supposed international benefits that could accrue in what is, first and foremost, an anarchic global order.

In sum, in the Liberal Institutional perspective, the very institution of the EU and its inherent formal arrangements may be the primary justifications for the hesitation of EU member states, simply because the aforesaid deliberations would not be necessary if the institution did not exist to bind the EU member states together.

B. *Constructivism*

The foregoing theory of Liberal Institutionalism presupposes that the EU member states, in hesitating to adopt the Singapore Convention, were doing so out of a constrained pursuit of their interests where they were acting out of a repressed attempt to find a course of action within the strictures of the EU which coincides with their individual objectives. In other words, the interests of the EU are prioritised, and the interests of the member states are simply a derivative of them.[19]

However, a converse interpretation of the impact of the EU on the actions of its member states may be found in the IR theory of Constructivism.

Applying this theory could present an alternative perspective — that EU member states were voluntarily acting in conjunction with their perceived identities constructed from their status as EU members.

Rather than using the language of "interests", Constructivism uses the language of "identities" to explain the actions of states. In this regard, "normative and ideational structures" shape the identities of states and influence what they consider necessary in decision-making processes. At the same time, states and the structures in which they are situated are "mutually constituted" — inasmuch as the structures construct the identities of states, the states' actions themselves contribute to the construction of these structures.[20]

From a state's perspective, the presence of the institution therefore defines, rather than constrains, their actions. Accordingly, decisions taken by these individual states adhere instead to a "logic of appropriateness", where states identify the social rules that are appropriate within the institution and consonant with their constructed identities, and act in accordance with them.[21] Put otherwise, the institution is essentially a source of "rules and practices that are socially constructed, publicly known, anticipated and accepted" by its constituent states, that both represent their identities and govern their decision-making processes.[22]

In exploring the impact of the EU on the identities of each of its constituents, it has been observed that their identities are so inextricably linked to and deeply defined by their status as EU members that they do not see themselves as discrete European states. Instead, their identities are constructed by and consist of the union's values of "'unity in diversity', democracy, human rights, the rule of law, and social market economy", and the subscription to the view that European law is paramount and the "law of the land".[23]

From this starting point, one could posit that EU member states expressed hesitation when presented with the Singapore Convention simply because doing so was a voluntary act consonant with their identities as EU members. The careful consideration of whether the EU should adopt the Singapore Convention as a union and the overt preference for the EU Mediation Directive may be perceived as a manifestation of the member states' respect of the primacy of the European legal order and the values of unity with which they identify. It is also unsurprising that they would perceive the prospect of amending their domestic European laws to bring them in line with the Singapore Convention as an affront to the primacy of European law, and in turn, their identities as EU members.

One can thus observe that the Constructivist perspective allows for a state to be seen as an inherently social actor making voluntary decisions. Instead of perceiving hesitation as a product of constraint by the overseeing institution, applying Constructivism to the situation would reasonably explain that EU member states were merely motivated by the desire to act from their perceived identities and thus reinforce the ideational structures constructing them.

C. *Structural/Defensive realism*

The common thread in the analysis thus far has traced the hesitation of EU member states in adopting the Singapore Convention as having roots in the institution of the EU. However, it may also be posited that their reticence stems instead from their individual concern of self-interest and relative gains vis-à-vis other states in the international system. This markedly distinct perspective may be gleaned from Defensive Realism, one of two strands of the broader theory of Structural Realism.

In stark contrast with the preceding two theories, Structural Realism generally posits that the international system is anarchic in nature, the prospect of cooperation is bleak, and states behave in rational ways in response to the constraints of this anarchic structure. One strand, Offensive Realism, takes the more extreme position that the primary response of states is to actively pursue dominance and hegemony so as to be secure in these strictures of anarchy.[24] The strand of Defensive Realism — which is the focus herein for its appropriateness to a situation where state competition is not overt — posits instead that the maximisation of security, maintenance of the status quo, and preservation of the existing balance of power are the guiding principles for state actions.[25]

In line with this, it has also been posited in Defensive Realism (in the context of military policies) that states which are satisfied with the existing balance of power may communicate their "benign intentions" to other states — that they are security-seeking and not power-seeking — by sending signals through the policies they choose to adopt.[26]

These tenets may be transplanted to the present situation to plausibly explain that the EU member states' hesitation to adopt the Singapore Convention is driven by their respective individual — albeit coincidental — desires to preserve the existing balance of power and the security inherent in the subsisting order. It is postulated that this security they seek to preserve emanates from two sources — the EU's place in the global economy, and its legal system.

In respect of the EU's place in the global economy, the EU is a heavyweight under the existing balance of power. In 2020, the EU had a GDP of almost US$15.3 trillion[27] and accounted for 14% of global trade, the second largest share only to China.[28] When faced with the prospect of strengthening the global economy at large by partaking in the Singapore Convention, it is not unsurprising for EU member states to consider instead that they may stand to gain more by adhering to the secure subsisting order, rather than entertaining the speculative possibility of an enhanced global trade network, as the latter may run the equal risk of upsetting the balance of power to their disadvantage. Under such circumstances, it would be reasonable to expect EU member states to engage in a considered analysis of whether a collective adoption of the treaty as an EU-bloc would maximise their security, which would explain the need for the deliberations in this regard and the hesitation generated as a result.

In respect of the legal system, EU member states may similarly find security in the well-developed "closed intra-EU system" for cross-border enforcement of MSAs established by a combination of the EU Mediation Directive and the Brussels I and II Regulations since 2008.[29] The individual states' domestic laws — which are modelled after these regional laws — adds a further pillar of strength to a well-entrenched, functional legal system. In this situation, it is again sensible for EU member states to prefer to remain rooted in this secure legal order, rather than to depart from it by adopting a novel global treaty and/or amending domestic laws as doing so unnecessarily introduces an element of uncertainty which could have the converse effect of jeopardising their guaranteed security.

Finally, it is not unlikely that the reticence exhibited by each EU member state is a signal sent to the other member states of its security-seeking intentions — which could explain the coincidental consonant response of all 27 states in the union. What appears to be a concerted response by all EU member states may instead be explained by Defensive Realism as a coincidental rational response to an inherently anarchic international system, rather than a consequence of being part of the institution of the EU.

IV. Conclusion

It can be seen from the foregoing theoretical analysis that a variety of plausible political reasons exists for the EU member states' hesitation in adopting the Singapore Convention. In choosing to exercise circumspection in signing on to this novel treaty, EU member states may have been acting within notional constraints imposed on them by the EU as an institution (Liberal Institutionalism), voluntarily desiring to adhere to the social rules in this institution which define their identities (Constructivism), or simply responding rationally to international anarchy by maximising their security which subsists in the status quo (Defensive Realism).

Unless and until clear official public statements are made to this effect, it is no mean feat to elucidate a firm explanation for the EU members' reticence in partaking in this novel global instrument. Nevertheless, the analysis above illustrates that theoretical underpinnings can provide an illuminating starting point for the investigation of this seemingly nebulous and puzzling phenomenon, which can in turn serve as a firm bedrock for a more considered deliberation of the matter.

https://doi.org/10.1142/9789811285257_0003

Keeping Confidentiality or Pursuing Transparency: The Dilemma of Transparency in Investor–State Mediation Mechanism

Fan Xiaoyu

Abstract[1]

As an important part of alternative dispute resolution, investor–state mediation is attracting increasing interest from the creators of investment treaties and institutional rules. Traditional mediation mechanisms are inherently confidential. Keeping mediation proceedings and related documents strictly confidential is crucial to successful mediation. However, investor–state disputes, which involve public interests, often do not allow for the strict confidentiality of traditional mediation. Rather, those involved in investor–state mediation face pressure to be transparent. To increase public acceptance and the perceived legitimacy of the investor–state mediation system, it is necessary to establish the right balance between confidentiality and transparency. The degree of transparency of investor–state mediation should generally fall between the strict confidentiality of commercial mediation and the transparency of investor–state arbitration. Distinct from investor–state arbitration and its exceptions to transparency and confidentiality requirements, investor–state mediation applies confidentiality in principle, with appropriately expanded transparency exceptions to respond to the need for transparency.

I. Introduction

In the context of investor–state dispute settlement ("ISDS"), mediation[2] is not new but has rarely been used.[3] In the last decade, however, the use of investor–state mediation ("ISM") has increased in the ISDS field, attracting growing attention from the creators of investment treaties and institutional rules. These and many other incremental changes and developments have allowed investor–state mediation and conciliation to gain momentum, but none of them have had a significant impact on practice. Among the commonly perceived problems and key obstacles to facilitating access to mediation[4] is the tension that remains between transparency and confidentiality under ISM.

Many scholars argue that the confidentiality associated with mediation could pose a threat to transparency, which is crucial to ISDS.[5] Strict confidentiality is one of the most important attractions and strengths of mediation.[6] However, when the government is named as the respondent, public interest calls for more transparency in the dispute resolution process.[7] The call for transparency applies not only to investor-state arbitration("ISA") but also to ISM. To address the criticism of 'secrecy', ISA authorities have begun drafting related reforms, including those allowing for public hearings, amicus participation, and the publication of awards and other informative documents. However, ISM lags behind ISA in terms of transparency.[8] A significant argument against the mediation of investor–state disputes is that it may be used to keep cases confidential and remove them from public scrutiny.[9] To maintain mediation as a valuable alternative, there is no choice but to respond to the increasing call for transparency and make adaptations to address these concerns. Striking a balance between confidentiality and transparency is necessary to integrate mediation into the ISDS mechanism.

However, to what extent would an increase in transparency in ISDS affect the generally confidential mediation process?[10] This article focuses mainly on the transparency issue as regards the ISM mechanism. Section II explains why ISM requires transparency from the perspective of theoretical analysis and practical reform. Section III discusses the role of confidentiality in the investment mediation world. Section IV provides an analysis of the tension between transparency and confidentiality in ISM. Section V discusses how to redesign guidelines to achieve the right balance between transparency and confidentiality under ISM. Section VI concludes the paper.

II. Importance of transparency in ISM

The drive for greater transparency in investment mediation stems from two main factors. The first is the public interest involved in investor–state disputes. The second is transparency reforms which have already been undertaken in the arbitration field. In light of these reforms, it seems inappropriate for ISM to remain highly confidential, as the high level of confidentiality could be used by parties as a tool to circumvent the ever-increasing standards of transparency in investment arbitration.

A. *Theoretical analysis of the characteristics of disputes to be resolved*

Investor–state disputes inherently involve public interests in several ways.[11]

On the one hand, investor–state disputes invariably involve a government as the respondent. As a party to such disputes, a democratic state must be accountable to its constituents for its decisions and actions[12] and subject itself to public scrutiny.[13] For some governments, there is also a legal duty to comply with domestic disclosure laws, such as the Freedom of Information Act in the United States.[14] In this way, transparency and participation contribute to good governance.[15]

On the other hand, an investor–state dispute always implicates the host country's public policies and public interests. Citizens of the host state have the right to know of and participate in dispute settlement processes regarding government actions that directly affect them. After all, the losing party to a lawsuit must pay considerable arbitration costs and awarded damages, which fees are ultimately borne by the taxpayers of the host state.[16]

B. *Transparency reform of ISA in practice*

ISA, the most popular instrument of ISDS, has been used to resolve all sorts of investment disputes on six continents for more than 30 years. That being said, many scholars have seriously questioned and criticised the confidentiality feature of the ISA system.[17] In this context, clear improvements in terms of transparency can also be witnessed in the practice of investment arbitration[18] and the norms of institution rules.[19]

III. Role of confidentiality in ISM

Most bilateral investment treaties ("BITs") are silent on the issue of confidentiality in ISM, and such matters are generally regulated by the applicable procedural rules. The importance of confidentiality is reflected in many ISM procedural rules, such as requiring that mediation sessions be conducted in private and that related information be kept confidential. Documents from mediation are not to be used for any other purpose in any other proceedings.

This high level of confidentiality is due to several factors. In terms of traditional practice, mediation thrives on the candour encouraged by strict confidentiality. Furthermore, confidentiality can address concerns about future repercussions, as documents from mediation cannot be used for other purposes. Confidentiality is one of the key institutional attractions of mediation, as opposed to the transparency of arbitration.

A. *Confidentiality status quo in ISM under institutional rules and international investment agreements ("IIAs")*

Many new institutional rules (including IBA, ICSID, ECT, ICC, IMI, and ARMO) and IIAs (such as CETA, EVIPA, and EUSFTA) suggest that ISM has entered a new phase in its development. These rules and agreements have made confidentiality a fundamental principle throughout the mediation process. The three characteristics of confidentiality observed in the current ISM mechanism are discussed below.

(1) *The confidentiality of the process*

Almost all mediation rules provide that all stages of the mediation proceeding are to be confidential.[20] This means that mediation sessions are conducted in private. Moreover, no persons other than the mediator, the parties, and their representatives are permitted to attend, hear, or view any part of the mediation, unless with the consent of the parties and with the mediator's permission.[21]

(2) *The confidentiality of the information*

The range of confidential information and documents is vast, and affected parties are subject to the obligation of confidentiality for a long period of time. For example, the new ICSID Mediation Rules state that "[A]ll information relating to the mediation, and all documents generated in or obtained during the mediation shall be confidential."[22]

(3) *The 'without prejudice' principle*

Generally, no information or documents related to a mediation are to be used for any other purpose in any other proceedings, particularly legal proceedings. The 'without prejudice' principle is reflected in many ISM rules[23] and is an essential part of the system design. It not only helps to maintain the confidentiality of mediation but also eliminates parties' concerns about the risk of leaking evidence in the ISM process.

B. *Why confidentiality is a vital component of ISM*

There are three reasons why confidentiality is so important to ISM.

Firstly, mediation thrives on the candour encouraged by strict confidentiality.[24] Investment disputes involve socially sensitive information, critical political concerns, major issues of public policy, international finance, states' international obligations, national sovereignty,[25] and issues that may not be effectively discussed in the public eye in general.[26] It is only in a confidential environment that the parties and mediators can frankly discuss the core issues of the dispute, the actual positions of the parties, their interests and concerns, and potential solutions. In this way, it is possible to successfully settle disputes and reach a settlement agreement through the mediation process.[27]

Secondly, confidentiality reduces parties' concerns about whether their candour could have repercussions for them in the future. To resolve disputes efficiently, parties may make some admissions of facts and promises, and the mediators may give some advice in the mediation. If a party were to be allowed to use the other party's admissions, offers of settlement, or expressed views or those of the mediator made during mediation as evidence in subsequent procedures, this would reduce the stability of the mediation procedure and hinder the fairness of subsequent procedures.[28]

Thirdly, confidentiality is one of the essential institutional attractions of mediation. Parties to investor–state disputes have a significant incentive to choose mediation[29] over arbitration, due to its many oft-cited advantages: it is cheaper and faster,[30] less formal, more flexible, and voluntary. The parties to mediation have control over both the process and outcome;[31] they can build trust and preserve their business relationship going forward.[32] Furthermore, they can consult with each other on economic matters beyond legal interests during the mediation process and fully express their respective claims. All of these advantages and others, which are crucial to the successful application of mediation, are supported by confidentiality.[33] It is precisely because the mediation process is not open to the public that it can resolve disputes in a relatively quick and cheap manner, and provide its users with tailor-made solutions.

IV. *Tension between transparency and confidentiality in ISM*

As previously stated, the many advantages of mediation are inseparable from the principle of confidentiality. A series of academic articles introducing ISM support the notion that confidentiality is essential to the survival of mediation.[34] The inclusion of confidentiality as part of the mediation process in the mediation rules mentioned above also demonstrates this. As Titi states, "It is difficult to envisage mediation that would work without the guarantee of confidentiality."[35]

However, confidentiality has also generated doubt and drawn criticism. Coe Jr. has argued, for example, that some would find a shift to mediation to be retrogressive in terms of transparency.[36] Hafner-Burton, Puig, and Victor agree, stating that "[the] major argument against settlement in ISDS is that it will be used to keep cases confidential and remove them from public scrutiny.'[37] Ubilava and Nottage have also commented that

> "...Due to this characteristic it has commonly been believed that mediation was not suitable for ISDS because public awareness and transparency constitute a crucial component of a dispute settlement regime where one of the parties is a state. Stakeholders in ISDS have expressed growing concerns that mediation will be used to bypass transparency[38] and also have access to universal enforceability through the 2019 UN Convention on International Settlement Agreements."[39]

This conversation raises the question of whether there should be a presumption of transparency in ISM.[40] Balancing the competing interests of transparency and confidentiality is essential for the mediation of investor–state disputes to flourish. Although it is challenging to reconcile the confidentiality of mediation with the public attributes of the state subject and the public interests of the disputed object in the investment dispute, it is only in this way can the feasibility and legitimacy of the investment mediation mechanism be improved, and the public's acceptance of, and trust in, the mediation operating system be secured.

V. Balance of confidentiality and transparency under ISM

A. *Essential positioning: confidentiality as a principle*

To improve the public's acceptance, or the perceived legitimacy, of the ISM system, it is necessary to establish the right balance between confidentiality and transparency. The principle of confidentiality should be adhered to, reserving disclosure as the exception. The ISM mechanism should be more confidential than investment arbitration, but it does not and should not reach the same level of transparency as commercial mediation.

As arbitration transparency standards gradually rise, maintaining the gap between mediation and arbitration transparency standards is necessary to maintain the advantages of the ISM system, including its greater likelihood of reaching settlements and its attractiveness to disputing parties. ISM has a number of advantages over ISA. Although confidentiality is important to an extent, due to the hybrid nature of investor–state disputes and public interest they entail, the transparency of investment mediation should be greater than that of general commercial mediation. With the inclusion of broader confidentiality exceptions, ISM can effectively respond to the current transparency reform trend by maintaining a level of transparency somewhere between that of commercial mediation and that of investment arbitration.

B. *Transparency in ISM*

Recently, some IIAs and institution rules have made attempts to better optimise mediation transparency while still balancing transparency and confidentiality. Rules which have been designed to maintain the essential characteristics of mediation confidentiality while allowing for some disclosure of information generally address private sessions[41] and confidential documents.[42]

It seems permissible for parties to disclose that mediation has been undertaken. Many institutional rules and international agreements applicable to mediation also appear to acknowledge that a strict confidentiality obligation should not extend to the fact that the parties have agreed to mediate, unless the parties agree otherwise in writing. Such rules include the IBA Rules for Investor–State Mediation, CETA's Mediation Rules, and the ECT's Guide on Investment Mediation.[43]

It also seems permissible under some rules to disclose the settlement agreement resulting from the mediation process. For example, the IBA's rules state that "[the] settlement agreement or part of its terms can be disclosed unless the two parties have agreed otherwise in writing."[44] CETA's mediation rules similarly provide that "any mutually agreed solutions shall be made publicly available."[45] Disclosing the settlement agreement resulting from mediation strengthens the legitimacy of the mediation in the eyes of the general public and shields public officials from potential criticism regarding the appropriateness of concessions or payments to the other party. It also facilitates the rebuttal of potential allegations that corruption was involved in the settlement agreement.

Institutional rules allow for an explicit listing of exceptions to the general principle of confidentiality. Potential exceptions to confidentiality can be found in the existing ISM rules. For example, the ICSID's newly released ICSID Mediation Rules stipulate three confidentiality exceptions,[46] although the confidentiality exception provisions in the IBA Mediation Rules are more detailed and illustrative.[47]

VI. Conclusion

The above analysis shows that due to the hybrid nature of investor–state disputes, it is necessary to maintain public interest and improve transparency for both ISA and ISM. However, due to their institutional differences, the two dispute settlement systems allow for different degrees of transparency. Through transparency reform efforts, ISA has adopted transparency as its principle and confidentiality as the exception, whereas the basic principle of ISM is still confidentiality, with reasonable exceptions of transparency. Although mediation is unworkable in some cases and therefore cannot replace arbitration entirely, ISM must successfully balance the requirements of transparency and confidentiality in order to offer an attractive complementary mechanism.

Given the public interest concerns, the ISM mechanism must be expanded to include more reasonable transparency exceptions while maintaining an appropriate level of confidentiality or it will lose its institutional advantages and value. Some international treaties and rule practices have made progress in this direction, but further optimisation will require countries to make choices based on their respective positions. The degree of transparency of mediation in a specific case should depend on the specific circumstances of the dispute, any transparency rules implicated in the relevant dispute settlement clauses, and the level of public interest and other calls for transparency involved.

The ISM mechanism is quite flexible in terms of transparency, allowing for a balance of confidentiality and transparency to be struck by the parties involved. Transparency is an increasingly important determinant of the development of the investment mediation mechanism. It will also affect the trends of both diversified investment dispute resolution and investment governance modernisation.

https://doi.org/10.1142/9789811285257_0004

Healing the Healer: It is Okay to Not Be Okay

Gini Wong Wei Wen

"Self-care means giving the world the best of you, instead of what is left of you."[1]

I. Introduction

Mediation has been described as a healing art. Beyond mediating the dispute(s) at hand, the mediator heals relationships between people.[2] To act as the so-called 'eighteenth camel',[3] mediators leverage a variety of mediation techniques to unlock the healing potential present within the parties at the mediation table. However, in the quest to empathise with others and mediate their conflicts, mediators may forget about their own self-care needs. The "levels of concentration and attentiveness" required of mediators, combined with the intensity of the situation, create conditions that are "both demanding and draining".[4] Behind the façade of being composed, patient, and empathetic, mediators do get tired and emotional. This may result in a condition known as burnout.

While much research has been done on the practice and process of mediation, a less-explored area is the needs of mediators themselves.[5] As Singapore rises to the forefront of the mediation field as a hub for alternative dispute resolution, it is important for the mediation industry to be aware of, and prevent, mediator burnout. This will help maintain and even enhance mediators' performance while taking care of them. Therefore, this essay seeks to answer the question: what is mediator burnout, and how does it impact the mediation process (apart from affecting the mediator personally)? Building on the above, this essay also proposes solutions for self-care, setting boundaries, and insulation.

II. Unpacking mediator burnout

At the outset, it is important to be familiar with the concept of burnout. Burnout refers to a state of physical, emotional, and mental exhaustion caused by long-term involvement in emotionally demanding situations.[6] In relation to burnout arising in one's job, there are three core components of burnout:

(a) exhaustion;
(b) depersonalisation (cynicism) by treating others one faces at work with an impersonal response; and
(c) reduced job efficacy and sense of accomplishment.[7]

Overall, the "universal lament of professionals suffering from burnout is, "I hate my job.""[8]

A. *Causes of mediator burnout*

A growing body of empirical research has shown that mediators are prone to burnout, which is caused by an amalgamation of various aspects of the job.[9] Two noteworthy causes related to the mediation process are emotional dissonance and mediators' own high expectations of themselves.

(1) *Emotional dissonance*

First, long-term emotional dissonance may contribute to mediator burnout. Burnout is frequently observed in professionals working in jobs that require 'emotion work', which involves personal contact with others and requires professionals to control their emotions.[10] Mediation undoubtedly falls into such a category. On the one hand, mediators are exposed to a broad range of emotions from the parties to the dispute, such as anger, dismay, denial, guilt and fear. On the other hand, mediators must remain impartial and neutral,[11] while developing a rapport and establishing trust with the parties. Hence, mediators must mask their true emotions, and may even "deliberately model" calm, positive, or empathetic emotions in the hope that parties will "buy-in to the mediation process".[12] However, it is impractical for mediators to not be personally affected by the parties' emotions or some of the information they become privy to in the course of mediation.[13] This results in emotional dissonance, which refers to the conflict between the mediator's experienced and expressed emotions.[14]

Let us take the example of a divorce mediation where the husband has alleged that his wife had cheated on him with a co-worker. During a private session, the husband tells the mediator that he knows that his wife did not have an affair, but wants the divorce because he is actually having an affair himself and does not want his wife to find out. The mediator may feel alarmed and perhaps even angry on the wife's behalf, but they must still appear to empathise with the husband despite any negative feelings they may personally be experiencing. Therefore, mediators must "be aware of, and constantly [regulate] their outward expressions to the parties" and suppress their innermost feelings.[15]

While this is especially so for highly emotional cases such as family, divorce, and community disputes, even disputes that appear impersonal contain emotional elements that the mediator must be attuned to. Over time, as the suppression of emotions takes energy, this eventually leads to exhaustion and detachment, which are core components of burnout.[16] Furthermore, burned-out mediators must "put more effort into emotional regulation than their unaffected colleagues". This in turn leads to greater levels of exhaustion.[17]

(2) *High expectation of themselves*

Second, mediators' high expectations about the ideal outcomes of mediation may lead to burnout.[18] Such expectations arise partly because mediation literature contains numerous stories singing its praises,[19] for example, describing mediation as having "magical moments when the right word or gesture (or even silence) unlocks seemingly intractable conflict".[20] Additionally, mediation has been touted to have high success rates, both locally and abroad.[21] Mediators may come to perceive mediation as a forum that always yields positive outcomes, and consequently develop high expectations of themselves in assisting parties to reach such outcomes.

For example, in a community dispute mediation between neighbours, a mediator may have an ideal of the neighbours reaching an agreement that allows them to have a 'happily ever after'. As a result of this, they may become driven by their own ideals and lose sight of what is realistic in the case at hand.[22] Despite the mediator's best efforts in facilitating the session, the neighbours may walk out of the mediation without resolving anything or worse, with greater hostility. Further, multiple attempts at mediation may also end in failure.[23] A frustrated mediator, after trying very hard to reach their ideal outcome, can become overwhelmed.[24] They may blame themselves and their competence (or lack thereof) for the mediation's 'failure', and also feel disillusioned about the purpose of mediation. When efforts do not yield the expected results, this may lead to exhaustion and eventual cynicism, which are core components of job burnout.[25]

B. *Other related concepts*

Burned-out mediators may also experience compassion fatigue and vicarious trauma. In understanding mediator burnout, it may be wise to keep these related, yet distinct, concepts in mind.

Compassion fatigue results from the cumulative psychological and physical effects of exposure to the pain, distress or injustice suffered by others, unlike burnout, which is usually due to work conditions.[26] Mediators may feel "fear, pain and suffering" because of their empathetic response from listening to the parties' stories and experiences.[27]

On the other hand, vicarious trauma occurs when professionals experience "painful images and emotions associated with their clients' traumatic memories". Over time, they may "incorporate these memories" into their own memories, causing trauma-based symptoms.[28] Here, mediators may develop vicarious trauma through listening to parties who retell traumatic or violent events.[29] For instance, in a high-conflict divorce case, the affected couple and their children may experience trauma-related symptoms such as insecurity and depression. Through interacting with the family and hearing (or even witnessing) the traumatic psychological and physical effects of the divorce on them, the personal crisis of the family may leave an 'imprint' on the mediator.[30]

III. Implications for the mediation process

Apart from negatively affecting the mediator's emotional and physical health,[31] mediator burnout also has implications for the mediation process.

Burnout impairs the mediator's cognitive functions in the following areas:

(a) "cognitive flexibility, or the ability to focus on multiple tasks simultaneously and to switch from thinking about one concept to another";
(b) "working memory, or the ability to take in new information, retain what is relevant, and discard what is irrelevant";
(c) the "ability to sustain or control attention"; and
(d) the ability to regulate and control their emotions.[32]

As the mediator leverages these cognitive functions throughout the mediation process and lends structure to how sessions are conducted, the quality of the mediation process greatly depends on them.[33] If their impaired cognitive function causes them to perform poorly, this, in turn, would affect the quality of mediation and mediation outcomes.

This section focuses on the implications of mediator burnout during the mediation session (although burnout may also affect pre-mediation conferences).[34] Specifically, the facilitative mediation process will be examined.

A. *Mediator's interventions*

Mediator burnout may diminish the mediator's ability to act as the 'eighteenth camel' in value-adding during the various stages of the mediation session.

(1) *Communication and information gathering*

Right from their opening statement, the mediator aims to build rapport and establish trust with the parties through verbal and non-verbal cues. A good relationship makes the parties feel understood and increases their openness towards the mediator and each other. To achieve this, the mediator employs techniques such as active listening (including to parties' non-verbal cues), summarising, questioning, reflection and reframing — all while appearing empathetic and non-judgmental and maintaining impartiality.

Once trust is established, using the analogy of an onion and its layers, it becomes easier for the mediator to 'peel off' the parties' outermost layer — their position — to uncover the deeper layers of 'interests' and 'needs'.[35] It is imperative to understand these underlying layers because a dispute is rarely simply about the matter in question but involves deeper concerns.[36] This also leads parties to be more open to different options during option generation. Consequently, the effectiveness of the mediator hinges on how well they can maintain both cool detachment and profound engagement with the parties.[37]

However, a burned-out mediator would struggle with the dynamic and multi-faceted aspects of the mediation process. Firstly, as depersonalisation is a core component of burnout, the mediator may end up viewing a particular mediation as 'just another mediation', causing them to fail to empathise with the parties. However, ignoring the emotional aspects that underlie a conflict reduces parties' trust in the mediator as they may feel that they are not being taken seriously. This may lead to a less effective peeling of the position-interest-needs 'layers'. Furthermore, the mediator may fail to 'peel' through these layers effectively using the relevant mediator techniques. For example, they may fail to ask 'tell me more' questions to understand the conflict or rush the discussion in a bid to end the mediation session earlier. This cuts short the discussion, which would otherwise have had so much potential for interest-gathering and getting to the root of the conflict.

Secondly, an exhausted mediator may struggle to regulate their emotions, keep biases at bay or avoid making snap judgments. Instead, they may end up relying on cynical or faulty heuristics to draw conclusions about a party's interests rather than engaging in further information gathering (e.g. "Just give this lady a chance to say her piece and hear an apology and this case will end").[38] This compromises the mediator's ability to deliver an ethical and high-quality process for the parties.

Thirdly, the mediator may overlook something crucially important or mismanage the exchange of information. For instance, mediators use reframing to encourage parties to see themselves or their dispute in a more constructive way.[39] However, as the burned-out mediator has reduced cognitive reflexibility and narrowed attention towards "local rather than global information", their ability to reframe would be compromised.[40] They may reframe the parties' statements in a different manner from the parties' intentions or their reframing may not be as eloquent in directing the parties to look at the bigger picture. A missed opportunity to capture a shared interest, correct a communication distortion, or shift parties' perspectives, could mean the difference between a breakthrough or a setback.[41]

Fourthly, the mediator may fail to notice power imbalances between the parties, such as where one party has more air time or sounds more aggressive than the other. In this situation, the mediator would not be able to limit the influence of stronger parties. This risks eroding the (weaker) party's trust in the mediator and in the procedural justice of mediation itself, because their perception of impartiality may be affected by the mediator's failure to intervene.

Fifthly, the mediator may fail to notice the parties' non-verbal cues, such as body shifts or gestures. As burnout can impair the ability of working memory to sort through auditory and visual stimuli, encoding relevant details and discarding the irrelevant, the burned-out mediator may miss visual cues that they would normally take as signs of hesitance or discomfort.[42] Left unaddressed, this could result in a party signing an agreement that they did not fully understand or was uncertain about.

The mediator's skills — empathy, patience, calmness and ability to help parties see things from a different perspective — are highly important, especially for disputes involving high levels of trauma or conflict (e.g., abuse, personal injury, family provision claims or family law matters). Burnout compromises these skills to the detriment of the mediation process.

(2) *Option generation and negotiation*

Crucially, burnout can affect option generation and negotiation. During these stages of the mediation process, the mediator supports the parties in coming up with a range of options for moving forward and assists them in making an informed choice through reality-testing each option. However, as burnout diminishes "creativity in problem-solving",[43] the mediator may not be able to evaluate the options effectively and probe the parties with critical questions to test their proposals. Additionally, they might stop asking the parties for additional suggestions, elaboration, or evaluation just because one option seems like a good one or the parties seem to have agreed on a course of action. By failing to delve deeper into each option, parties may eventually agree on a course of action without thinking much about its feasibility — and may come to regret it afterwards. Moreover, given the reduction in their cognitive flexibility, the mediator might face difficulties with making a mental map of the big picture while listening actively to the parties' conversation and linking them to the issues. In this way, burnout can limit the value-add that the mediator brings to option generation and negotiation.

B. *Parties' emotions*

A burned-out mediator's negative emotions may also infect the parties at the mediation table. If the mediator shows difficulty in regulating their emotions and expresses negative emotions such as exhaustion, the parties may notice it. This is significant as research into neuroscience has shown that the mediator's thoughts, intentions, and emotions matter on a very "subtle, yet profound level".[44] Specifically, mirror neurons present in our brains play an important role. When we observe others, these mirror neurons fire up and send signals to our limbic system, which allows us to feel the emotions associated with the observed facial expression or behaviour.[45] As a result, the burned-out mediator's negative emotions and body language may cause the parties to subconsciously 'mirror' their negative emotions. In such a situation, the mediator would not be able to build rapport with the parties. As parties would be more hostile and less collaborative, the mediation session may not be effective in resolving the dispute overall. Furthermore, the parties may lose trust in the mediator and the mediation process if they sense hostility or disinterest on the part of the mediator.

IV. Solutions

The above points demonstrate how mediator burnout compromises the quality of the mediation session and does a disservice to the parties in mediation. As the best treatment is always prevention, it is crucial to prevent mediator burnout. In any event, there should be adequate support for mediators experiencing burnout.

A. *Self-care and empowerment*

It is essential for mediators to learn how to practice self-care — before, during, and after a mediation session — to prevent burnout and cope with symptoms. Self-care comes in many forms, but it fundamentally allows us to focus on ourselves — as millennials say, 'putting me first'. Self-care techniques are especially important when mediators begin to feel that stressors are taking a toll on them to prevent this escalating into burnout.[46] As proper training on self-care strategies and adequate knowledge on burnout can be effective preventative measures,[47] it is imperative for organisations to hold trainings and workshops which focus on mediators' emotional needs.[48]

For example, mindfulness strategies such as meditation and yoga can be incorporated into these trainings.[49] Mindfulness refers to the mental state of being present, where an individual connects their thoughts, feelings, and bodily sensations and roots them in the present moment.[50] Mindfulness can benefit mediators greatly, such as by helping them improve their patience, remain calm in the presence of conflict and make them more aware of their own emotions.[51] This allows mediators to stay focused and present during the mediation session while keeping a certain distance from their own emotions. Mindfulness techniques can be practised before, after and during the mediation session. For example, during the mediation session, if the mediator feels overwhelmed by the parties' emotions, they can use mindfulness breathing techniques to help them stay calm and focused.

Overall, these are some points that trainings should cover:

Training point	Purpose
• Prepare mediators for the intense emotional experiences that they will encounter during mediation sessions • Prepare mediators to have a realistic understanding about how *far* mediation and mediators can help parties • Teach mediators to release attachment to the mediation outcome — the mediator should not be working harder than the parties in coming up with a settlement	• Allow mediators to understand the realities of mediation • Manage mediator's expectations towards themselves and the mediation process
• Introduce mediators to the concepts of burnout, compassion fatigue and vicarious trauma • Teach mediators to understand that feelings of burnout and the related concepts of compassion fatigue and vicarious trauma are normal	• Increase awareness on these issues, and prevent stigmatisation
• Teach mediators, such as through case studies and role-plays, how to handle highly emotional situations during the mediation session • Teach mediators how to stay sufficiently detached yet empathetic to a case — mediators should not be excessively invested in a case emotionally. • Encourage mediators to practice holistic self-care — physical (*eg*, sufficient rest, regular exercise), mental (*eg*, meditation, engage in hobbies), emotional (*eg*, personal therapy, trusting relationships) • Introduce mindfulness tips and strategies for mediators to practice before, during and after mediation sessions	• Prepare mediators to understand and manage their emotions, and also parties' emotions • Teach mediators burnout prevention and coping strategies

B. *Support*

The mediation community and mediation organisations should also play a role in helping mediators develop emotional resilience.

Firstly, it is recommended that mediation organisations or interest groups create support groups for mediators as these groups can provide "a safe professional arena for troubleshooting and for maintaining a balance".[52] Having support helps decrease mediators' isolation and even diminishes feelings of shame about experiencing burnout.[53] Mediators can also learn and reflect from others' experiences and coping strategies. While some may think that such support groups violate client confidentiality, they can still function in ways that do not betray this. For example, mediators could simply talk about their emotions and general experiences rather than bring up a particular case or client.

Secondly, mediation organisations can implement or strengthen their mentoring systems, especially for mediators who deal with cases involving high conflict and trauma.[54] Co-mediation may also be another solution (although it can present its own set of stressors).[55] These steps may help mediators when they feel solely responsible for addressing daunting and highly distressing problems. Moreover, with a more collaborative environment, colleagues can help recognise early on if a mediator is experiencing burnout and provide support thereafter.

V. Conclusion

Mediators often proclaim that mediation is "much more of a calling than a job".[56] Indeed, the art of mediation can be a healing and rewarding experience for both mediators and the parties, but passion can only take mediators so far.[57] Burnout is an insidious condition that affects both the mediator and the mediation process. Therefore, to heal others, mediators must first heal themselves.

https://doi.org/10.1142/9789811285257_0005

Navigating Two Different Truths in Family Mediation: One Size Will Not Fit All

Neo Xin Xuan

I. Introduction

> "The confidence people have in their beliefs is not a measure of the quality of evidence, but of the coherence of the story that the mind has yet to construct."[1]

The above quote by bestselling author Daniel Kahneman aptly encapsulates the idea that different truths can co-exist. While our experiences, aspirations and fears are the tools for this process of construction, psychological biases hinder our perception of an objective reality.[2] Indeed, truth is relative in mediation — as it is in life.[3] Consequently, a mediator's goal is never to get parties to agree on one view of a past incident, but to bring parties *past* the incident and focus on future dealings with each other.[4]

This paper seeks to examine the role of the mediator in family disputes, who is required to skillfully navigate the different truths of two parties coming out of a failed marriage. Mediators have to appreciate that when a couple has decided to file for a divorce, they are perhaps at the most highly conflicted point of their lives.[5] Nothing is as highly emotionally charged as the process of going through a divorce — be it due to the couple's grief over the breakdown of their marriage, or because their pride and ego are also at stake. Crucially, the latter also affects ancillary matters such as the division of the matrimonial assets and custody battles.[6]

It is during family mediation that people with high conflict personalities ("HCPs") most often appear. Often, it is these HCPs, rather than the issues per se, which drive conflict and hostility in family disputes.[7]

Given the high likelihood that parties involved in family mediation have HCPs, this paper posits that a mediator has to adopt a different approach when dealing with such individuals. Instead of leaning towards handling the mediation based on how parties *ought* to behave, mediators have to understand and recognise these HCPs *before* they can employ appropriate strategies to better work with these individuals and protect the mediation process.[8] In fact, mediators who have training and experience in the mental health profession find that their diagnostic formulations of HCP individuals aid their functioning as mediators.[9]

II. 'Double-hatting' in family mediation

Do family mediators also act as therapists? Surprisingly (or not), this is a frequently asked question due to the similarities in goals, techniques, and outcomes between mediators and therapists.[10] Notably, while mediation is compulsory for divorcing couples in some countries, it is possible that therapy could better serve some divorcing couples than the mediation process.

A. *The grey area*

It goes without saying that emotions run high in both mediation and marital therapy settings. Apart from dealing with the substantive issues of the dispute, an effective family mediator would also address parties' psychological issues and reactions to the dispute.[11] In this sense, there are overlaps between these roles in having to handle how the parties express and explore their feelings.

Furthermore, the effects of mediation might, in some cases, overlap with those of therapy. Mediation may improve communication between some couples, allowing them to experience a reduction in anxiety and an increased acceptance of the divorce.

B. *Key differences between mediation and therapy*

(1) *Goals*

While exploring the emotions tied to the dispute may help parties move things forward, the goal of mediation is neither to help parties resolve their grief over the marriage ending nor to turn the sessions into marital therapy. Mediation is very much a problem-solving process with regard to the divorce and the relevant post-divorce matters, with the ultimate goal of reaching a settlement agreement. By contrast, therapy seeks to expand, rather than contain, psychological exploration.[12]

In the likely event that there is too much conflict, causing the parties' emotions to 'hijack' the mediation process, mediators have to make continuous, dispassionate judgements about how much emotional expression and exploration is really needed.[13] The mediator should be able to navigate the emotions verbalised by the parties and reframe their emotionally charged language to allow the mediation session to progress. This signposts the importance of the mediator's role, which will be discussed further below.

(2) *Process*

Mediation has a clearly delineated structure that is tailored to its being a goal-focused, task-oriented, time-limited process.[14] Parties are made aware of the mediator's process and intentions before agreeing to participate. The realistic 'needs' of the respective parties, or rather, their interests — the buzzword in mediation — undergird this process.[15]

By contrast, decisions in therapy are based on how one feels.[16] The therapy experience is more subjective, where the intrapsychic issues and emotional needs of the couple gradually unfold as more sessions go by. To facilitate this process, the therapist encourages parties to explore the meanings and levels of dysfunctional psychological reactions.[17] The opposite is true for mediation, where too much conflict can destroy any progress that has been made. Further, clients in divorce cases are often less tolerant of any negative emotions and may decide to cease mediation altogether.

III. Dealing with high conflict personalities

Family mediation is unique in the extent to which it has been derived and synthesised from diverse fields of practice.[18] The family mediator not only has to understand the law and legislation governing family matters, but also be skilled at dealing with conflicts. The mediator must both understand how people react and have the ability to react appropriately when there is conflict. Indeed, it is common for jurisdictions to require mediators to undergo additional training to enhance their skills in managing family disputes before they can become accredited family mediators.

Having established that there is the grey area between the roles of therapist and mediator, this paper posits that a certain degree of acknowledgement and exploration of feelings is needed in mediating family matters. In doing so, the mediator leverages certain skill sets which overlap with that of a therapist. While mediators cannot be expected to help end all anger, by recognising the influence HCPs can have on a dispute, mediators will be better prepared to help move the mediation session forward and ideally towards a beneficial settlement for the divorcing couple. However, professionals involved in such high-conflict cases often exacerbate the situation by failing to understand that there are personality traits and characteristics that explain why individuals refuse to disengage and get along.[19]

While this presupposes that the mediator should already know how to identify HCPs, this paper does not endeavour to analyse these personalities in detail or discuss their impact on the mediation process. Instead, this paper is angled from the mediator's perspective in terms of how mediators can best protect the mediation process and serve the interests of the divorcing couple when dealing with individuals with HCPs. This paper focuses on the relevant skills a mediator should have in dealing with individuals with HCPs, due to their potential to tie up the mediation process with endless complaints and declarations and heighten the conflict.[20]

In his book "High Conflict People in Legal Disputes", Eddy identifies five different types of HCPs, namely paranoid, histrionic, narcissistic, borderline, and anti-social.[21] A key characteristic of individuals with HCPs is that they have a target of blame and are driven by their cognitive distortions, causing them to focus all of their frustrations and anger on their target and worsen the conflict.[22] In the mediation setting, this target is often the HCP's spouse, whom they perceive has betrayed them. This may manifest in various ways. For example, the individual with the HCP may lie to the mediator in an effort to shame or paint the target in a bad light, in an effort to get the latter to change their behaviour. Crucially, individuals with HCPs often have no regard for the impact their destructive behaviour has on others (and the mediation process).[23]

Just as the personal qualities of the parties may influence the mediation process, the same can be said of the mediator. It is therefore important to recognise the role and techniques of the mediator in dealing with individuals with HCPs in family mediations, as neglecting to do so would only look at half the picture.[24]

A. *The role of the mediator*

As Eddy has stated, "[Like] a teacher separating kindergarteners on the school yard, a mediator must be willing to cut off reflections about who pushed whom first, and instead, focus on how to play nicely."[25] The role of the mediator is not to enter a fact-finding process and point fingers or decide on liability, but to bring parties beyond the events which have transpired and focus on how to "play nicely", ideally through reaching a settlement agreement.

Mediators are referred to as neutral third parties who do not make decisions for the couple, but are limited to facilitating their decision-making process.[26] Indeed, impartiality is an ethical requirement of mediators.[27] That being said, one cannot undermine the role of the mediator, whose mere presence can affect the way parties behave during mediation.

This is similar to the phenomenon known as the "Hawthorne effect", which refers to the behavioural changes people make when they realise that they are being observed.[28] Given the sensitive nature of the topics that arise in family mediations, parties might feel safer pursuing these topics in the presence of a third party.[29] Furthermore, it may be more productive to have a neutral party facilitate discussions between the couple (for example, if the divorce was due to the discovery of infidelity in the marriage). A possible explanation for this might be the power imbalance which often exists between divorcing parties, a point which will be discussed further below. What is significant here is that mediators can, by their mere presence, influence the parties. As such, what more might trained mediators, who are equipped to deal with HCPs, bring to the table?

Separately, the role of a mediator can be considered from a systems perspective. The dynamics between parties involved in the mediation process are also explored in Gestalt psychology, which asserts that all living organisms must not be perceived in terms of isolated elements, but as a whole.[30] In the mediation setting, this phenomenon would be comprehensible only if the whole set of interactions between the parties and the mediator, the qualities that each brings to the process, and the changes wrought by those interactions, are considered in totality.[31]

For these reasons, mediators need to constantly remind themselves of their influence over the mediation outcome due to the control they exert over the mediation process,[32] giving rise to the need for mediators to constantly hone their skills and techniques.

B. *Techniques of the mediator*

Understanding the human condition is as important, if not more so, in the mediation process than in other dispute resolution mechanisms. Mediators can employ several strategies to prevent individuals with HCPs from hijacking the mediation process and help parties to make progress.

(1) *Power balancing*

In 75–80% of cases, the decision to separate is a unilateral rather than a mutual one, and it is common for one spouse to have a continuing emotional attachment to the other.[33] This leads to a power imbalance between the parties, with the party initiating the divorce having an upper hand over the mediation process. Because of this, it is essential for the mediator to remain neutral — particularly when mediating disputes involving HCPs who can be very persuasive in blaming others.[34] The dynamics of such a power relationship (with the HCPs dominating) may put additional strain on the parties, causing further disempowerment and harm to the party being "dominated".[35]

The mediator can influence the power balance by encouraging respectful communication, ensuring that parties get equal talking time, and adopting an even-handed approach to the parties.[36] Conversely, the mediator has to be careful to avoid inadvertently exacerbating the existing power imbalance by imposing impartiality on an unlevel playing field.[37] Taken together, however, these statements present a paradox: to prevent one party from dominating over the other, the mediator should intervene to try to balance the process,[38] but at the same time, mediators are expected to stay impartial and support clients' self-determination. This can be viewed as tension between client self-determination and fairness, two values which rank very highly in mediators' ethical framework.[39]

To reconcile this conflict, which is seemingly inherent in the role of a mediator, the key question to ask is: how neutral should a mediator be? In seeking to answer this question, we will find that the mediator seeks to balance both parties' interests in every mediation, albeit to different extents, depending on the circumstances surrounding the mediation at hand. Consequently, while the 'power-balancing' role of the mediator seems to contradict or detract from the beauty of mediation, which seeks to appeal to the idea of neutrality, it really exemplifies the intricate role of the mediator.

While the power dynamics in each mediation may be complex, and the concept of 'balancing' power fraught with difficulty, many aspects of process design, strategies and interventions can be employed effectively by mediators to ensure that parties are able to negotiate effectively and reach fair outcomes.[40] Furthermore, given that power is based on perception,[41] the mediator becomes even more important in regulating the ever-changing power dynamics between parties in a mediation.

(2) *Silence*

As French composer Claude Debussy famously said, "Music is not just about the notes, it is about the space between the notes." The same principle applies in mediation, where silence may well signal that some important reflection is going on in the minds of the parties, allowing the mediator to be very creative in the mediation process. Mediators should learn to grapple with absolute silence when resolving conflicts and resist the temptation to jump in and say something. Rather, they should let silence be their friend.

In family mediation cases involving individuals with HCPs, parties may reach an impasse due to the HCP individual's attempts to dominate the mediation process. In such a situation, apart from suggesting that parties explore private sessions, the mediator could simply stay in the moment and do nothing, waiting until someone eventually says something. Allowing the silence to fill the space gives the HCP individual an opportunity to reflect and be more aware of their own emotions.[42] Otherwise, without these periods of silence to "promote self-reflection and cool tempers",[43] they are less likely to become aware of the consequences of their destructive behaviour on the mediation process.[44] Silence may also facilitate a pause from the intensity of the mediation process, allowing time for HCPs to shift their thoughts to a completely different subject matter.[45]

Early studies in human communications and family therapy have established that all interactions, even those where there is a failure to communicate, constitute a form of communication.[46] Accordingly, silence from one party can communicate a certain message to the receiving party.[47]

Clearly, there are different sorts of silence. In family mediations involving HCPs, silence may arise due to embarrassment or anxiety, perhaps about what the listener may construe. Conversely, silence can also give the parties time to think and to build trust.[48] This being said, it may be appropriate for the mediator to avoid intervening prematurely and allow the parties to sit in silence focusing on the quality of the silence and the extent to which it appears to be comfortable, beneficial and meaningful for the parties. The mediator should continue to engage in active listening and intervene if the HCP individual chooses to use the silence destructively, working with them to increase their emotional intelligence.[49]

(3) *Time travel*

Mediators are often looking at a slice of the parties' lives where they are not at their best — they might be highly emotionally roused, angry or hurt. This applies to both parties, whether they have HCPs or not. As mentioned earlier, HCPs tend to be persuasive at placing blame on another party– but why do they feel better when they do so?

This is because HCP individuals often have it backwards: they are unable to see their own part in disputes, and therefore cannot help to solve the problem.[50] The HCP indivdual tends to think their problems are external, rather than internal, and often feels distressed and helpless when their target of blame does not change. The party on the receiving end, conversely, would undoubtedly feel hurt by the actions of their ex-partner.

To break out of the HCP's pattern of being unable to reflect on their own behaviour and denying responsibility for their part in causing the conflict, the mediator could direct the parties to reflect on what they were like at a time *before* the dispute.[51] This encourages the parties to 'time-travel' beyond the particular moment when the conflict arose — perhaps to a time and a place where they were able to work things out or communicate in a different way.

IV. Conclusion

Mediators play a key role in identifying and managing difficult behaviours presented by the parties in mediation. The majority of family matters in mediation involve an intense, high level of conflict which is often driven by the party with a HCP.[52] Instead of applying a fixed mindset, mediators should use an evaluative approach without losing their neutrality towards the process. Mediators should recall that individuals with HCPs are often defensive, and it is therefore incumbent upon them to defuse this by balancing the process, inviting silence, and encouraging parties to 'time-travel' beyond the point of the conflict.

https://doi.org/10.1142/9789811285257_0006

The Fundamental Concept of Voluntariness in Mediation: Is Mandatory Mediation an Oxymoron?

Ng Xin Ying Nicole

There has been a concerted move towards the use of mediation as a key dispute resolution mechanism in various jurisdictions, including Singapore, where mediation is viewed as a complement to the adversarial litigation process. The promulgation of the new Rules of Court 2021 ("ROC")[1] introduces amendments that reinforce Singapore's stance in promoting amicable dispute resolution, including mandatory mediation. In light of these changes, it would be appropriate to examine the legitimacy, effectiveness and desirability of court-mandated mediation, which remains an objectionable proposition for some commentators.

At first glance, it may be surprising that mandatory mediation continues to face resistance given the aforementioned global trend towards mediation. However, there are arguments against court-mandated mediation on the grounds that it appears to contradict the voluntariness of the process, which is widely considered to be a fundamental aspect of mediation. On the other hand, there are several compelling reasons for mediation to be compulsory. Oftentimes, the voluntariness element is also not completely removed. At the root of the issue lies a delicate balance between the parties' right to choose and the important bases on which mandatory mediation is founded. This balance may be tipped in either direction, depending on public policy considerations, legal culture and the judicial system of a country.

As a starting point, there are various forms of mandatory mediation. A distinction may be drawn between what has been termed as categorical referrals, where a statute explicitly provides that certain classes of disputes have to be referred to mediation, and discretionary referrals, which relies on judicial discretion to determine whether mediation would be appropriate in a particular case.[2] An example of categorical referrals is mandatory counselling and mediation for all divorcing parents with any child(ren) below 21 years of age.[3] For discretionary referrals, the court may order parties to attempt amicable dispute resolution, according to Order 5 Rule 3(1) of the new ROC. Moreover, the level of compulsion in a court-mandated mediation exists on a "continuum".[4] On one end of the spectrum, there may be a requirement to consider mediation as a dispute resolution option (e.g., Alternative Dispute Resolution ("ADR") Form 6A).[5] Taking this one step further are "soft" penalties such as adverse costs orders for unreasonable refusals to mediate (e.g., Order 21 Rule 4(c) of the new ROC, read with Order 5 Rule 1(4)). At the other end, there is direct compulsion where mediation is explicitly required before the commencement of legal proceedings, without any option for parties to "opt-out" (e.g., compulsory pre-action protocols for non-injury motor accident, personal injury, medical negligence and defamation claims).[6] Within this continuum of court-mandated mediation, the element of voluntariness has been circumscribed to varying extents.

I. Voluntariness in mandatory mediation

Voluntariness has consistently been touted as one of the core tenets of mediation. An emphasis has been placed on the notion that "all parties must agree to use mediation" and any agreement to resolve their dispute must be reached "voluntarily".[7] Consequently, mandatory mediation has primarily been resisted on the basis that it is antithetical to the voluntary nature of the process.

In response to this, it has been suggested that a distinction may be drawn between compelling parties to enter into the process of mediation and compulsion within the mediation itself.[8] This would justify court-mandated mediation if parties are only required to attempt to reach an agreement to resolve their dispute but cannot be forced to achieve an outcome.[9] With respect to the aforementioned continuum of court-mandated mediation in the Singapore context, parties are merely told to try mediation and always have a right to decline settlement, regardless of which end of the spectrum their mandatory mediation may lie. During court proceedings, the terms of an offer for amicable dispute resolution and the reasons for refusal to attempt mediation may not be examined by the courts until after the determination of the merits of the case.[10] Since the parties are free to walk away from the court-mandated mediation without compromising the merits of their case, the essence of voluntariness is retained. As the saying goes, "you can lead a horse to water, but you cannot make it drink".[11] Indeed, the entire mediation process has to be free of coercion, even though parties may be urged to take the first step in entering into it.

However, the threat of sanctions, including the imposition of adverse costs orders for unreasonable refusals to undergo mediation, has the potential to blur the lines between compulsion *in* and compulsion *within* mediation.[12] Due to fear that they will incur cost penalties during later court adjudication should they decide not to settle, the parties may indirectly be compelled to reach an agreement containing "terms that are less than acceptable or fair" to them.[13] Under the new ROC, the court has the power to not only disallow or reduce a successful party's costs, but also order that party to pay costs,[14] if he or she has acted unreasonably, failed to make an offer of amicable resolution of the dispute or rejected such an offer without reasonable grounds to do so.[15] The question is: to what extent will the court scrutinise the process in reviewing whether the parties behaved unreasonably?[16] If the court has the power to impose cost penalties in view of a party's unreasonable conduct during the mediation itself,[17] this may compromise the essential aspect of confidentiality and produce a chilling effect on the mediation process.

On the flip side, it may not be wholly objectionable to impose cost penalties on parties for their unreasonable conduct. It is not uncommon for a party to be penalised for their failure to follow civil procedure rules. For instance, default judgment may be entered against a defendant who has failed to serve his defence within a given time frame.[18] Since mediation is complementary to the adjudication process and forms a part of Singapore's civil justice system,[19] court-mandated mediation or amicable dispute resolution may simply be considered as just another step that parties have to comply with. Furthermore, cost penalties should be imposed to deter parties from unduly wasting judicial time and resources, which is ultimately a public good. Nevertheless, it seems that if the sanctions to be imposed in lieu of an unreasonable refusal to mediate are overly punitive, or parties' communications are subjected to rigorous scrutiny by the courts, the fundamental principle of voluntariness may be infringed.[20]

In addition, the civil procedure rules do not explicitly state what constitutes "unreasonableness", completely leaving it up to the court's discretion. This allows the court to have some flexibility in examining the particular facts and circumstances of each case, preventing court-mandated mediation from succumbing to the over-generalisation that mediation is suitable and appropriate for every single dispute within a certain category.

As mentioned earlier, divorcing parties who have at least one child below 21 may be ordered to undergo mediation and counselling.[21] Despite this, the court also has the power to dispense with such an order if it considers that it may not be in the interests of the parties or their children to attend mediation or counselling.[22] An example is where family violence has been committed or where Child Protection Services is involved in the case.[23] The broad discretionary powers of the court have to be exercised in a way that ensures the protection of victims of domestic violence within the legal system, rather than subjecting them to "face-to-face mediation with the person from whom they are fleeing".[24] Therefore, it is envisaged that the court will take into account the nuances of each particular dispute, rather than being overly paternalistic or dismissive of the valid reasons a party may have for refusing to participate in mediation.

The examination of reasonable grounds for refusal to mediate nonetheless begs the question: should the mere fact that parties do not wish to mediate with the opposing party be a valid reason in and of itself? In other words, should parties be given the right to choose their dispute resolution mechanism? Since people have the capacity to make decisions about their relationships with others, they should also have the free choice not to undergo mediation. This argument emphasises party autonomy and self-determination, implying that mediation has to be free of compulsion to the extent that even entry into the mediation process must be completely voluntary.[25] However, a counter to this is that the court possesses the inherent power to regulate its own procedure. The new ROC acknowledges that the court can do whatever it deems necessary to ensure that justice is done or to prevent an abuse of process.[26] Hence, it is fully within the case management process and adjudicatory power of the courts to compel parties to mediate their dispute.

Court-mandated mediation may also be rationalised as a "temporary expedient" to encourage widespread use of mediation and give people the chance to experience the benefits of amicable dispute resolution.[27] This is necessary because the uptake of mediation has been slow, despite its documented advantages.[28] To borrow Randolph's analogy, if mediation and litigation were products sold at supermarkets, people would queue up to purchase litigation (which they know is costly, lengthy and risky) while leaving mediation (the cheaper, faster and less risky product) on the shelf.[29] Although the adversarial system pits parties against each other in a hostile environment and leads to prohibitive costs and time being incurred, parties and their lawyers remain uninformed or are unfamiliar with mediation as a viable alternative.[30] Additionally, a party may be unwilling to initiate mediation or make an offer for amicable dispute resolution, out of fear that such a move would be perceived as a sign of weakness by the other party.[31] As a result, disputants often fall back on litigation as the default option. Hence, it is argued that some degree of compulsion is necessary to educate parties and help them overcome their prejudices or lack of understanding of what mediation entails. Court-mandated mediation brings public awareness and attention to the process and allows mediation to begin to develop as a real alternative, so that parties do not unnecessarily enter into prolonged litigation.[32]

II. Access to justice in mandatory mediation

The concept of voluntariness is necessarily linked to the discussion of whether court-mandated mediation contravenes the rule of law — in particular, the right of parties to have their day in court and access to justice. In 2021, the UK's Civil Justice Council ("the UK CJC") released a report examining the legality and desirability of compulsory alternative dispute resolution.[33] In particular, it discussed the controversial decision of

Halsey,[34] where it was held in *obiter* that imposing mediation on unwilling parties would "impose an unacceptable obstruction on their right of access to the court", thereby violating Article 6 of the European Convention on Human Rights ("ECHR"), i.e., the right to a fair and public hearing within a reasonable time.[35] Nevertheless, the UK CJC has concluded that mandatory mediation would only contravene parties' Article 6 rights if it is "disproportionately onerous" or forecloses "the parties' effective access to the court".[36]

In *Halsey*, Lord Dyson opined that the right of access to a court can only be waived if the party is not subject to constraints, giving the example of an arbitration agreement as a valid waiver.[37] It is submitted that mediation cannot be compared to arbitration, the outcome of which is a final decision that is binding on the parties. In mediation, parties retain the right to go to court in the event that mediation is unsuccessful and their access to courts is delayed rather than completely denied.[38] It is likely that *Halsey* was based on a misconception that ordering parties to go to mediation was equivalent to ordering them to settle, when in reality, settlement is to be reached voluntarily and there can be no compulsion within the mediation process. When parties have the unfettered right to start or resume litigation if an agreement is not reached in mediation, Article 6 of the ECHR will not be violated.[39] However, a caveat to this is that the deferral of parties' rights to go to court should not be draconian in nature.[40] This may be found in Article 6 itself, which states that the right to a fair trial must be within a "reasonable time". At any point during a court-mandated mediation, parties must have the right to walk away from the process and go back to the courts.

Amicable dispute resolution methods, including mediation, have been criticised for facilitating "more access to less justice",[41] in that the focus on achieving settlements impedes the ability of the justice system to deliver just and accurate results. However, it is submitted that the basis behind parties getting their "day in court" may be conceived as the fundamental right of parties to be heard. Mandatory mediation has become an important component of the judicial system that supports the rule of law by allowing for justice to be achieved outside the confines of the courtroom.[42] The process of mediation creates a safe space for parties to listen to and communicate with each other, bringing them closer together so that a more constructive outcome can be reached. In particular, parties are encouraged to come up with creative solutions tailored to their particular situation by looking towards the future, as opposed to litigation, where they focus on the wrongs they have suffered in retrospect.[43] Contrary to the argument that court adjudication and mediation are "diametrically opposed" dispute resolution mechanisms, they actually complement each other in a way that allows fair and just outcomes to be achieved.[44]

Litigation is a tempting option for parties who, driven by their indignance or hurt, seek "complete vindication, outright success, public defeat and humiliation of the other side".[45] However, fighting a legal case based on sheer "principle" or the "vindication" of one's rights can prove to be extremely costly.[46] The reality is that protracted litigation is a daunting process for disputing parties. Many litigants, even if victorious, leave the courtroom feeling unsatisfied because they did not get what they truly wanted. By contrast, the mediation process potentially creates "greater party satisfaction" due to its ability to explore parties' deeper interests and offer a range of solutions that are not available to the courts, including apologies.[47] Moreover, it would be incongruent for parties to go to court for a claim that would amount to or be disproportionate to the costs that they incur. As Chief Justice Menon aptly puts it, the "best system in the world is useless if it cannot affordably be accessed by those who need it".[48] As such, increasing the use of mandatory mediation would threaten neither the existing adjudicatory system nor traditional legal rules.

III. Effectiveness of mandatory mediation

Last but not least, the effectiveness of court-mandated mediation has been heavily doubted. It is presumed that since parties were compelled to undergo the process, they would be unwilling to negotiate past their impasse, thus leading to an unproductive mediation where settlement cannot be reached. However, in practice, this assumption has not played out. Even when parties are compelled to mediate, rates of settlement have been high and parties generally find the process to be beneficial.[49] In recent years, the rate of settlement for Supreme Court cases in Singapore that had been referred to mediation ranged between 66% and 81%.[50]

This is likely because a well-trained mediator has the ability to "close a large gap" between the parties or make them "see sense".[51]

Where settlement is not reached, mandatory mediation has been criticised for being an additional obstacle to the parties' access to justice by exacerbating costs and delays against their will.[52] Nevertheless, it is submitted that mediation can be desirable and effective even without a settlement. By undergoing the mediation process, disputing parties gain a greater understanding of the issues in dispute as well as each other's interests.[53] Consequently, litigation commenced at a later stage will be better streamlined to manage any residual difficulties.

IV. Conclusion

In conclusion, mandatory mediation is not only legitimate, since it does not contravene the rule of law or any fundamental human rights of the parties, but also effective, as the process may result in productive outcomes despite parties' initial reluctance. As the mandatoriness of mediation lies on a continuum, "all mediations are voluntary, but some are more voluntary than others".[54] Since court-mandated mediation may be conceived as a temporary expedient that seeks to educate the general public and encourage uptake of the process, it seems that some degree of curtailment of the parties' freedom to enter into mediation is necessary. The benefits of mediation and its essential value as an amicable dispute resolution mechanism may make it justifiable to impinge on the voluntariness aspect of "front-end, participation", as long as "back-end, outcome" consent continues to be present.[55]

Ultimately, a cost-benefit analysis must be taken, as any discussion about the legality and desirability of mandatory mediation is heavily dependent on one's view as to whether voluntariness is so fundamental to mediation that it cannot be circumscribed in any shape or form. It may be that mediation remains the most appropriate method of dispute resolution in certain contexts, such as neighbourly disputes, where emphasis is placed on fostering harmony within the community,[56] or family disputes, where a child's needs take foremost priority.[57]

In Singapore, the balance has mainly been tilted in favour of mandatory mediation, since disputants do not have absolute freedom to choose whether they want to participate in amicable dispute resolution processes. The reason for this may lie in Singapore's history and culture, since mediation has been "deeply embedded in Asian culture" since ancient times.[58] Generally, there has been a tradition of village headmen, clan associations and community leaders using informal mediation to resolve disputes, that is consistent with, *inter alia*, Confucian values and Islamic principles.[59] The Singapore judiciary has thus made a concerted move to revive the usage of mediation in the legal system.[60]

Ultimately, at the heart of the debate over the voluntariness of mandatory mediation, or the lack thereof, there are important public policy considerations which have been informed by the legal culture and judicial system of each particular jurisdiction.

https://doi.org/10.1142/9789811285257_0007

In Pursuit of Therapeutic Justice: Mediation and Singapore's Family Justice System

Tan E-Shane Christabelle

I. Introduction

We often hear that the principle of therapeutic justice ("TJ") undergirds the practice of family law and how disputes in this realm are resolved, including in the Family Justice Courts ("FJC"). While therapeutic justice has generated much writing and discussion, at the same time, it seems hard to pinpoint what it refers to exactly. From the introduction of elements of therapeutic justice into the family justice system, till its formalisation as part of the vision of the FJC,[1] collaborative and non-adversarial methods like mediation and counselling have remained inextricably connected to the conception of family justice in Singapore.

The use of mediation in resolving family-related disputes is not unique to Singapore. A simple Google search of "family justice and mediation" pulls up multiple references to family mediation being used in other jurisdictions like Canada, New Zealand and Australia, just to name a few. However, Singapore's model can be distinguished as the FJC provides mediation services within its Family Dispute Resolution Division (the "FDR division"), which can refer parties to mediation. Therefore, mediation and Family Justice in Singapore boasts a much closer connection – or a much more top-down involvement, in that sense.

In this paper, I will firstly attempt to introduce therapeutic justice and locate it among the broad goals of the family justice system in Singapore. Next, I will cover how mediation is part of this process, first by expounding on *why* mediation, and subsequently, *how* mediation promotes the aims of family justice in Singapore. Finally, I will go into the potential downsides of the current model in which mediation is employed, and suggest alternatives or improvements because, as with all things, the Singapore model needs to be evaluated critically for its pros and cons.

II. Therapeutic justice and the goals of family justice

Therapeutic justice is, simply put, the methodology of looking at cases via a "lens of care" approach, which seeks to keep a keen eye on how laws, decisions, and legislative landscapes have a very real and in some cases, harmful and disparaging, effect on actors[2] in the family justice system. It therefore refers broadly, to how to best improve the system — in a forward-looking sense — but when it comes to cases at hand, it concerns itself with ensuring that parties involved are not caused any further hurt or harm on top of the dispute itself. At the very least, it seeks to reduce any further hurt that is caused as far as possible.

This less abrasive and more nurturing approach is required as, from first blush, it will be easily appreciated that disputes before the FJC are of a very different character from civil or even criminal cases. They involve more sensitive situations and people who, in some cases, have been present in each other's lives for decades. It is therefore understandable and in fact expected that emotions can run high, given the personal and relational stakes involved in such cases — not least where there are children involved. In cases involving children, the welfare of the child is the "first and paramount consideration",[3] which cannot be departed from. Further, it is worth noting that the standard to which the FJC finds the welfare of the child is "ubiquitous", which emphasises FJC's commitment to ensuring that children do not face massive disruption due to the divorce proceedings.

Therapeutic justice hence eases parties who enter the family justice system into the next phases of their lives in the following ways:[4] by protecting families and children (in terms of keeping their welfare the foremost consideration), by helping families adjust to their new circumstances, and finally, by empowering and providing support to these new family units, especially in co-parenting efforts, so as to minimise disruption to their children. Such a non-adversarial approach — significantly, one that seeks to ensure minimal harm is done to relationships and the individuals who pass through the system even when litigation might be involved[5] — therefore underscores the FJC's commitment to ensuring that overall, parties emerge well-supported and having avoided additional hurt.

III. How mediation ties into the family justice system

Having laid out the goals of therapeutic justice as a model that undergirds the family justice system, it is therefore not a stretch to consider how mediation fits into this framework. Since mediation is a model of dispute resolution, or sometimes, a step towards dispute resolution that focuses on examining the interests of each party and accordingly, generating options and looking at what best fits both of them,[6] it comports well with the vision of family justice in Singapore and its theme of amicable, minimally disruptive conflict resolution.

A key feature of mediation that makes it suitable for use in the FJC — being aligned with its goals and therapeutic justice as a whole — is that it allows parties to retain more autonomy than if litigation were involved. Parties have a say as to when to enter into the mediation and the issues to be tabled for discussion, and are allowed airtime to convey their thoughts in a candid manner to the mediator, an impartial third party.[7] This entire process is one where both parties are actively involved and engaged with each other as facilitated by the mediator, in a collaborative effort to iron out disagreements. Since this process is also largely flexible and the mediator is given room to decide how to interject, guide the discussion, or conduct the session itself, mediation therefore presents itself as a healthy, safe space[8] to foster open and honest conversations about crucial issues such as custody and maintenance.

Another factor that is closely related to the parties' autonomy is that they have a say in the outcome of mediation — i.e., in terms of any settlement that is reached or even in the key milestones leading up to a settlement. As opposed to litigation, where the judge determines the outcome, mediation allows parties to contribute and have their voices heard and represented in the eventual outcome. Ideally, this is one that satisfies both parties.[9] This is especially crucial in cases involving families and children precisely because of the sensitive nature of the subject at hand, building on years of relationships and ties that bind people who live, breathe, and hurt. Going through this process and seeing their opinions translated into a settlement agreement, should one arise, serves to ensure that parties adhere to what is agreed upon.[10] Significantly, such an agreement is also reached without acrimony and instead in the spirit of collaboration underpinning therapeutic justice, with the children's welfare at the forefront and facilitated by the mediator.[11]

As previously described, Singapore's family justice system approaches mediation slightly differently from some jurisdictions in that there is much more official support or connection to the use of mediation by way of the FDR division, and for mediation as a course of action. To be clear, parties with a child or children who are below 21 years old have to undergo mandatory mediation at the FDR division to resolve disagreements that may arise over maintenance, the divorce itself, living and care arrangements (custody), and the division of the matrimonial assets and property.[12] Notably, in the spirit of therapeutic justice, there is mandatory counselling for the parties in such cases as well.

Apart from the stipulation to undergo mandatory counselling and mediation in cases involving children, the FJC has the power to refer parties to the FDR division for mediation in other conflicts.[13] These include, but are not limited to, divorce and ancillary matters not involving children and applications under the Guardianship of Infants Act, Adoption of Children Act or Mental Capacity Act. As a whole, we can see how mediation, has been heavily incorporated and made readily available for parties who are dealing with family disputes in the hope of achieving a peaceful and amicable resolution to their problems, as far as possible. I describe mediation as a tool that is readily available as, even in cases where the court has *not* referred parties to the FDR division for mediation, parties still have the option to request for mediation at any stage of the process, whether through their lawyers or not.

This reinforces the inseparable nature of mediation and the brand of family law Singapore's family justice system seeks to promote and operate — i.e., one that ensures that parties respect and get to hear each other out, with the help of the mediator as an impartial third party who can provide a fresh perspective to deadlocked disagreements. Having the safe space to talk, and a mediator involved to facilitate, helps keep parties on track in ensuring the welfare of any children remains paramount.

Having a say in this process via mediation is hence beneficial as it safeguards the healthy involvement of parties, and encourages fidelity to the courses of action that arise out of the agreements from these sessions.

IV. Critiquing the current model and suggestions

As with all things, however, there are always two sides to a coin, and nothing is ever completely good or completely bad. The closely interconnected nature of mediation and Singapore's family justice system can be also said to be one of its downsides. In particular, the mandatory mediation requirement and the FJC's power to refer parties to mediation under the FDR division can ironically bring about inflexibility and further stymie conflict resolution.

One of the key limbs of mediation is that it is a voluntary process that both parties have to agree to enter into. As such, the idea of mandatory mediation or a mediation that parties are directed to attend seems to violate this very idea and the spirit of mediation in itself. This argument about the intended characteristics of mediation aside, mandatory mediation also raises practical considerations. In instances where parties might not be willing to come for mediation but are forced to do so regardless, they could be uncooperative and impede the process. At the furthest extreme, the parties could become vindictive in their dealings with the mediator and each other.

Reluctance to commit to the process or half-hearted involvement is not only dangerous and detrimental to the outcomes of the mediation itself. It also greatly discourages the other party and potentially hampers the relationship, or any hope of a future collaborative relationship, where the other party is legitimately invested in the mediation process. Where there are children involved, an unhappy or hostile experience at mediation, might pose difficulties to co-parenting plans in terms of impasse and deadlock (i.e., if both parties refuse to cooperate and see each other's perspectives). This directly goes against the goals of therapeutic justice in the realm of family law in Singapore, which prioritises the welfare of the child.

The idea that the child's welfare should be of paramount importance, cannot be divorced from the concept of healthy co-parenting. "Taking an extreme example of a case where parties are both uninterested in mediation, as mentioned above, they could act vindictively to one another out of spite and sheer refusal to cooperate." This would cause more vitriol and unhappiness between the parties, who might further anger and offend each other in turn. The divorce proceedings would therefore become incredibly acrimonious. Such a process runs counter to what the FJC seeks to achieve via its endorsement of, and reliance on, the FDR division and mediation.

While alternatives and improvements can be suggested, because critiquing and pointing out potential pitfalls is not enough, it must be acknowledged that such alternatives are hard to come by and have to be properly contemplated. A balance has to be struck between offering everyone a chance at mediation (even those who are uncertain about its efficacy from the start), and ruling it out for those who enter already intending to stymie the conflict resolution process, or who would more likely complicate matters further with their reluctance to cooperate.

A possible way to strike such a balance would be to include an opt-out option for parties, where parties who have objections to participating in mediation are allowed to make these known. This can be combined with some sort of system to assess the viability of mediation for each pair before they are even sent for it — for example, by way of assessing the parties themselves alongside their case to deem if they are likely to pose a major threat to the mediation process or the development of any future relationship with each other. While this ensures that mediation would only serve those who truly intend to iron out their disagreements, such a procedure also risks denying people the opportunity to undergo mediation based on conclusions and evaluations that were made about them and their cases.

For instance, parties who are rather on the fence about mediation might be identified as being unsuitable for mediation, whether for fear of stymieing the case or to protect the already damaged relationship. "However, there is the very legitimate possibility that if given the opportunity to try mediation out, it could very well reap positive outcomes for them." A way to tackle this would be to have personnel from the FDR division take the parties (who are given the option to consider mediation, opt out of it, or be assessed for their suitability for it) through the mediation process and be on hand to answer questions, like a case manager of sorts. However, a pertinent (and very Singaporean) concern that comes with this is whether it might slow down the process. The attention to detail needed to ensure proper checks are done would require more manpower and may result in longer wait times, which is likely to face opposition in efficiency-obsessed Singapore.

This is not to say that we should give up considering ways to improve the system altogether. Just because something is working now — in this case, the current model of the family justice system and its deep reliance on mediation — does not preclude considering ways in which it can be further improved, in the hope of giving rise to outcomes with minimal disruption to children and families. While neither the principal consideration of the welfare of the child, nor preserving a healthy relationship between co-parents and parent to child, can be departed from, these cannot be treated as an indication that mediation should always be sought, especially where it is clear that prolonging the parties' conduct could very well be what causes further distress.

The dedication to holistic, healthy and therapeutically-aligned justice, and hence a preference for mediation, should not be an open invitation to trample on and take advantage of its mild nature. While it is true in some sense that mediation is less formal than litigation and more desirable in terms of cost savings, this does not mean that it should be abused as a platform for spiteful and petty vindication between parties. It is suggested that the balance between encouraging mediation, and not forcing it where it is unsuitable, is one that has to be struck carefully and re-evaluated constantly so as to ensure this fine line has not been encroached upon or worse still, abused.

V. Conclusion

The FJC's dedication to therapeutic justice and the overarching idea of a healthy, minimally damaging resolution process for family disputes is a noble and needed one, as family law disputes involve multiple parties, many of whom have had deep connections for years on end and whose lives are about to change overnight. While it is understandable, in light of this, that the FDR division emphasises mediation in the hope of ensuring continuity and amicable discussions between the parties, we also must remain cognisant that there are times where mediation simply would not be sustainable or suitable.

Striking such a balance will be an ongoing task. While the model of mandatory and court-referred mediation — which pushes people towards mediation even where they prefer not to — might have its benefits, alternatives and ways to improve it bear serious consideration. Much as the popular saying goes, "if it ain't broke, don't fix it", there is a difference between repairing and enhancing something — and we can always, always find room for improvement.

https://doi.org/10.1142/9789811285257_0008

Children Should Be Heard To Be Seen: Including Children in Divorce Mediation

Tan Pei Han

I. Introduction

In divorce mediations, especially those which concern issues of custody and care, the best interests of the children are at the forefront of the discussion. However, in these mediations, it is typically the parents who gather to negotiate care arrangements. Two questions then arise: 1) who decides what the child's best interests are, and 2) is it self-defeating to assume that the interests of the child can be represented by their parents? Furthermore, by inviting parties to decide on what is "best", is there a possibility that this encourages competition, as opposed to cooperation?

Is the concept of the "best interests of the child" then one of complementary or competing interests, legitimacy, commitment or something else entirely? This is difficult to answer in any exclusionary manner, especially if this concept has been set as a goal of mandatory mediation in law; its overarching nature in family law means that sometimes it is hard to take another perspective of divorce and co-parenting arrangements. Yet, parents, children and mediators all have different considerations in conceiving what these best interests are.

This paper seeks to explore the inherent advantages and disadvantages of "the best interests of the child", as well as the relevance of including children in divorce mediation. Part II will examine the complications of considering both the child's and parents' interests in divorce proceedings. Part III will examine how the "best interests of the child" is used as a principle of legitimacy and an argumentative resource for either party when they disagree with the other's parenting styles. Part IV will examine the benefits of hearing from children at mediation. Part V concludes that while including children in mediation may not resolve the aforementioned issues, a focus on separating children's interests from their parents' may lead to clearer, more targeted discussions.

II. Complicating child's and parent's interests

A. *Established law in Singapore: joint parental responsibility as in the best interests of the child*

The "best interests of the child" can be found in the United Nations Convention on the Rights of the Child (UNCRC). Article 3(1) states that "In all actions concerning children, whether undertaken by public or private social welfare institutions, courts of law, administrative authorities or legislative bodies, the best interests of the child shall be a primary consideration." Singapore, having acceded to the UNCRC in 1995, likewise places the best interests of the child at the forefront of its family law. It is relevant to first begin with the hard law, where there is abundant jurisprudence regarding what the Singapore courts conceive of as the "best interests of the child", before delving into family mediation, which judges may mandate under Rule 22(3)(a) of the Family Justice Rules 2014.

The idea that joint parental responsibility is an essential safeguard of the best interests of the child is deeply rooted in Singapore's family law. Part 6 of the Women's Charter (Cap 353, 1997 Rev Ed) provides for the rights and duties of both the husband and wife, and sets out at the very beginning in Section 46(1) that both parents are mutually bound to cooperate in caring and providing for their children. In the seminal decision of *CX v CY*, the Singapore Court of Appeal interpreted that the welfare of the child "is best secured by letting him enjoy the love, care and support of both parents".[1] By equating a child's best interests with their parents' duty to provide and care for them, the concept of the child's interests becomes entangled with the parents' rights and duties to run their own households.

Naturally, there are exceptions to the idea of joint parental responsibility, but these exceptions are often in the extreme — for example, where one parent has died or if one parent has exhibited abusive behaviour towards the child. Where the parents merely have an "acrimonious" relationship, the court would still order arrangements that involve joint parenting. Ultimately, by prioritising the involvement of both parents, the court is working off the assumption that joint parenting is necessarily in the best interests of the child.

Case law provides an elaboration on this assumption. In *VJM v VJL and another*[2], Debbie Ong J stated that "a parent will need sufficient amounts of regular and frequent time *with the child* to build a strong relationship *with the child*" and to "bond and create many positive memories *with the child*"[3] (emphasis added). Here, the court takes the perspective of the parent's needs, stressing the preliminary interests of regular and frequent access to the child. From the way the quoted sentences are constructed, the child almost seems like a passive participant, even if they too will benefit from having a strong relationship and positive memories with their parents. In short, the interests of the parent and the child are assumed to be strongly intertwined, such that the fulfilment of the parent's interests is taken to mean the fulfilment of the child's interests as well.

B. *Conflating the interests of the parents with the interests of the child*

To be clear, there is nothing egregious about this conflation — the assumptions that parents and children share the same interests generally appear sound. The aim of joint parenting is to provide a secure transition for the child by minimising the loss they suffer (be it a familiar home or a parent) and reducing the emotional burden they might face due to "a conflict of loyalties".[4] In making decisions for the child, joint parenting ensures that both parents' perspectives are taken into consideration, thus benefiting the child when there is comprehensive input into how such a choice is made.[5]

What is of note, then, is the fact that such conflations make the phrase "in the best interests of the child" a loaded one. It is easy to forget that parents also have their own interests that may not be in the best interests of the child, or that there may be multiple styles of parenting that fulfil the best interests of the child. For instance, the Singapore High Court in *TAU v TAT* ("*TAU*")[6] recognised that there were other considerations in coming to a working arrangement for the care of a child post-divorce. The court drew a distinction between the idealised conception of child-care arrangements (i.e., joint parenting as being equivalent to the child's best interests) and "the realities, including the parental conflict, the parties' emotional baggage and the new dynamics of the various relationships".[7] This recognition of parents as not simply existing as caregivers of their children, but also as individuals in a partnership, is important as it clarifies the final caregiving outcome as a balance of considerations that take into account the diversity of parenting arrangements. At the same time, it also serves as a reminder that parents should not be judged harshly for having interests and limitations outside of their children.

The High Court in *TAU* also noted that arrangements should be tailored to "that particular child's needs at that stage of life" and "whether it is easy for that child, bearing in mind his or her age and personality, to live in two homes within one week".[8] The former goes towards the child's interests, suggesting a focus on the specific present and not some nebulous overarching ambition that parents may conceive for the child. In a similar vein, the latter goes towards both the ideas of comfort and convenience for the child as well as the feasibility of the arrangements in terms of how they are received by the child, rather than how they are managed by the parents. All these return the focus on the child's best interests to what is felt and understood by the child, as opposed to what parents wish for their child or a general standard or ideal of parenting.

In mediation, where the interests of the parents are more easily fleshed out, this problem of conflation should not arise. Yet, it is easy to envision the ways in which it could. For one, acknowledging their own "parental feelings" could "lead to accusations of being selfish".[9] It could also lead to the parent being identified as being "irrational";[10] where the "best interests of the child" is an ever-present source of legitimacy endorsed by the law, parents may feel compelled to project their own interests onto the child.

It is easy for parties to agree that it is in their common interest to emphasise the welfare of the child, and even overwhelmingly easier to assert that whatever outcome is reached should be guided by the "best interests of the child" — even though this principle fluctuates with social trends while also being deeply personal to the specific child in question.

III. The best interests of the child as a principle of legitimacy

Legitimacy, measured by way of objective criteria, is commonly used to introduce the notion of fairness in the mediation. When there is a conflict between parties' interests, one way of resolving this is to refer to objective criteria, such as the market value of an asset or legal precedent.[11] Still, there are limitations to the element of legitimacy, such as where "there are no objective criteria by which to gauge likely outcomes", or where the objective criteria is uncertain.[12] In such situations, parties are likely to adopt a positional approach to negotiation.

Where the overarching purpose of the divorce mediation is to ensure the welfare of the child, however, the parties may feel that the notion of fairness does not take them into account. Children are always seen as innocent parties to the divorce. They do not (often) participate in proceedings and are therefore absent from the mediation. With no say in the divorce, the child is already in a position of 'unfairness'. Should either parent object to an arrangement for the reason that they find it personally unfair, the objecting parent may be seen as derailing the mediation from its goal of ensuring fairness for the child[13] if not being outright selfish. Consequently, the "best interests of the child" becomes the *de facto* objective criteria, and fairness for the parties is parked under this umbrella concept by way of emphasising differing parenting strategies.[14]

Furthermore, competing sources and expert positions may be involved in determining the "best interests of the child". Adding to the complication of defining this objective criteria is that such generalised research may not apply to every child in question. Where it may be instinctive to suggest, for example, that a third party carry out a valuation of shares in a commercial mediation, it is counterintuitive to suggest that parents leave the interests of their child to be decided by a party with no connection to the case. Moreover, where the parties come armed with competing sources about what should inform the child's welfare, deciding on how these objective criteria should be defined becomes a battle of persuasion.

A further problem is that it becomes easy for the mediator to appear to break neutrality or impose their judgement on the parties. Mediators are required to draw on common ground between parties, especially to build rapport where there may be hostility. In divorce mediations, they are tasked with focusing the discussion on the child's welfare. However, any missteps by either party to frame their proposal as the preferred parenting arrangement could be seen as a deviation from this. Where the mediator tries intervening neutrally by referring the parties to the common objective (e.g., by asking if the proposal is in the best interests of the child), one party may latch onto this criteria as an "argumentative resource" to discredit the other.[15] Of course, this can be remedied by introducing more objective criteria (i.e., the standard of fairness) into the mediation — which itself can create more complications if there is a need to prioritise the standards for example.

IV. Benefits of hearing from the child in mediation

A. *Right of the child to be heard*

The right of the child to be heard in legal proceedings can be found in Article 12 of the UNCRC. Where the child "is capable of forming his or her own views", they should be accorded "the right to express those views freely in all matters affecting [them]".[16] The weight given to those views is to be "in accordance with the age and maturity of the child."[17] Article 12(2) of the UNCRC outlines the ways through which the child's views should be heard in judicial and administrative proceedings, whether "directly, or through a representative or an appropriate body".

In Singapore, the child's views are typically heard indirectly. Under Part V — Alternative Dispute Resolution of the Family Justice Courts Practice Directions ("the FJCPD"), children are generally not included in mediation or counselling even when the issues discussed are about them. Direction 12(4) of the FJCPD states that "[c]ounsel and parties are expected to come [to the Family Dispute Resolution Conference] prepared to discuss all issues relating to or impacting the child or children". Direction 13(4) gives counsellors the discretionary power to involve children in the counselling sessions, as well as discretion over how they should be included — for example, whether in a separate session from their parents or together with their parents.

These methods of hearing from children (as filtered through their parents or the counsellor) mean that there is no guarantee that their views will be heard and reflected accurately, even on issues that concern their interests directly. Understandably, however, it may be against the child's welfare to directly include them in mediation sessions. For one, children may not have the appropriate authority to settle. Secondly, mediation may be indistinguishable from court or administrative proceedings, and thus adds pressure on children to 'pick sides' so that a settlement can be reached.

B. *Benefits of including children in mediation*

There exist more inclusive approaches to hearing children in mediation. For instance, one method of child-inclusive mediation is for the mediator to speak to the child without their parents present, and then repeating the child's views to the parents at a separate mediation session. It should be noted that in 2015, the Singapore Child Focused Resolution Centre offered a pilot Child Inclusive Dispute Resolution model to 20 families.[18]

One of the benefits of hearing from the child at mediation is that it ensures their interests are communicated directly, thus increasing the specificity of discussion in mediation. Where the child's "direct experiences" are not expressed, "the power of parental projections and inaccurate assumptions" about the children had "greater license to continue unchecked".[19] On the other hand, where the child's voice is introduced through an independent, neutral third party such as the mediator, the parents' assumptions can be corrected immediately and the discussion refocused on specific examples of the child's experiences.[20]

Further, the authority of the mediator can give weight to the child's opinions, creating space for the parents to actively engage in discussing what the child felt. This could combat some of the common problems plaguing parents' interpretation of their child's opinions. For one, the child's views may be seen as immature or short-sighted and thus deemed inferior to the parents' more experienced assessment. As such, their views may not be properly represented at mediation when it is the parents who control how those views are represented, if at all. Furthermore, the representation of the child's opinions by either parent at mediation may cause one party to feel that the child's opinions have been tainted by the other parent's own biases. These run the risk of neglecting the child's own perspective. On the other hand, the mediator is a professional who is tasked with controlling the process. Their impartiality and lack of personal interest in the settlement can give the impression that the child's opinion is authentic, objectively felt and worthy of consideration.

Finally, parents may feel more inclined to accept the child's opinions when they are presented by the mediator, even if they do not align with their own assessment.[21] The role of the mediator is to conduct 'reality-testing' for the parties, such that they can freely assess the viability of their solutions without feeling like they have to concede on any point. This ability of the mediator to provide alternative perspectives empathetically, even where these may run completely counter to a party's views, encourages parents to consider opposing views from their children without fear of being judged as an uninvolved parent.[22]

By making the mediator the main conduit of information about the child's perspective, this reduces the possibility of parents competing to provide an anchor on the child's opinions. Removing a possible situation where one parent may appear to know more about their own child than the other "levels the playing field" for both parties.[23]

V. Conclusion

Due to its widespread use, the concept of the "best interests of the child" carries the burden of legal interpretation. Its judicial interpretations give an impression that there is an ideal, correct way to create arrangements that serve the child's best interests. Further complicating this ambition is the fact that while the parents are present at mediation, their interests are secondary, and children are usually not present at mediation although their interests take centre stage.

It may not always be feasible to have children's voices reflected at mediation; they may be too young to express a view, may not want to express their views at all, or there may be a shortage of trained mediators to help facilitate this. Worse, it may be the case that parents do not recognise their children's views as relevant or worthy of consideration even after they have been shared by the mediator. Nonetheless, even if mediation in such cases may be doomed to fail anyway, there is no harm in introducing children's views on issues that will materially affect them. Generally, when children are consulted in the making of a decision, they are more likely to feel more comfortable with the outcome.[24] At mediation, airing children's views independently from their parents may be important in allowing parents to share their own interests, allowing for greater clarity regarding the different factors contributing to the final settlement arrangement.

https://doi.org/10.1142/9789811285257_0009

Challenges to Ratification and Practice of the Singapore Convention on Mediation in China

Tao Chongyang

I. Introduction

On 12 September 2020, the United Nations Convention on International Settlement Agreements Resulting from Mediation ("the Convention") entered into force.[1] The Convention is a milestone in the history of the international commercial dispute resolution system. It marks the transnational enforceability of international mediation agreements and makes the international commercial mediation system an independent remedy for international commercial disputes in addition to litigation and commercial arbitration.

Giving enforceability to an international mediation settlement agreement has a jurisprudential justification distinct from that of a mere contract. Compared to an arbitral award, the parties have more control over a mediation settlement agreement, with the scope to not only agree on the resolution procedure but also its substance. This indicates that the parties accord a special status to the mediation settlement agreement. Although many countries consider mediation agreements to be contracts, they are in fact given even more respect than contracts. On the one hand, the parties give up some of their litigation rights in the mediation process in exchange for the other party's prompt performance of their obligations; on the other hand, the parties spend time and financial costs in mediation. If they reach a new contract, but the dispute remains unresolved, this would fail to satisfy their reasons for choosing mediation in the first place. From the perspective of institutional design, if the mediation agreement is more often confirmed through judicial confirmation to determine its effect of blocking new procedures and obtain enforcement through judicial confirmation, this minimises the potential illegality of the mediation agreement, but interferes with the parties' autonomy and increases the burden of judicial review accordingly. On the one hand, this makes it impossible to improve the efficiency of dispute resolution. On the other, it reduces the significance of mediation as a dispute resolution method.

The birth of the Convention has improved the protection of international commercial conciliation in the existing international legal system. In practice, if the parties fear that a settlement agreement might be torn up, they usually need to go through certain procedures to confirm the validity and enforceability of the agreement, such as converting the settlement agreement into an arbitral award or a judicial decision, and then seeking the protection of the 1958 New York Convention or the Hague Convention on Choice of Court. However, this practice may not be universal and effective. Based on the shortcomings of the existing international legal system, it is essential to create a new international convention to ensure the validity and enforceability of commercial settlement agreements.

In the context of encouraging and promoting the development of the international commercial mediation system, China has signed the Convention but has not yet ratified it. As such, several questions arise. Firstly, what are the differences between the mediation provided for in the Convention and under the Chinese mediation system? Secondly, should China ratify the Convention, and if so, when? Finally, how does the international commercial mediation system fit into the Chinese judicial system?

II. Challenges to the ratification of the Singapore Convention on Mediation in China

In China, settlement agreements resulting from an institutional, organisational, industrial, lawyer, and court-appointed or commissioned mediation involving international commercial disputes may fall under the scope of the Convention. The Convention is also applicable to mediation agreements involving international commercial disputes in litigation and arbitration, where the final legal instrument reached is not enforceable as a judgment, ruling, or arbitral award. Therefore, the Convention has great practical applicability in China, but at the same time, there is some resistance to ratifying the Convention when the current Chinese mediation system is taken into account.

A. *Lack of enforceability of international settlement agreements resulting from mediation in China*

According to China's Civil Procedure Code, a settlement agreement reached after mediation by a commercial mediation organisation, an industry mediation organisation, or other organisations with mediator functions has the nature of a private contract. The parties may jointly apply to the People's Court to confirm the validity of the settlement agreement, and the settlement agreement may be enforced by the court after judicial confirmation.[2] At present, the Supreme People's Court has expanded the judicial confirmation procedure to include mediation by chambers of commerce and mediation by lawyers.[3] Thus, in China, mediation agreements (including international mediation agreements) are civil contracts recognised by mediation organisations or institutions and are only given enforcement after certain forms of judicial review. Unlike the theoretical understanding and judicial practice of mediation agreements in China, the Convention gives direct enforceability to international mediation agreements. Theoretically, the enforceability of an international mediation agreement arises from the Convention, but if it needs to be enforced by the state, it has to be reviewed by the enforcement agency, which is an inherent requirement for the state to exercise its enforcement powers.

At the international level, enforceability is used as a characteristic of international settlement agreements because having enforceability would create a misconception in some countries that the agreement is *res judicata*. Under the Convention, only a few substantive issues, such as the formal elements and public policy of an international settlement agreement, can be examined by the competent authorities at the enforcement stage. The Convention creates the legal effect of direct enforcement of international mediation agreements, while under China's current legal system, foreign or international mediation agreements need to be transformed into court judgments, rulings, or arbitral awards before they can be enforced. Thus, (i) clarifying the legal nature of international settlement agreements and (ii) making the parties recognise the independent remedial function of international settlement agreements are the core issues that need to be addressed for the ratification of the Convention in China.

(1) *No practical background for individual mediation in China*

Mediation has both institutional and individual forms. For a long time, China has implemented an exclusive institutional management model for mediation. One thing that needs to be emphasised is that such mediation institutions are both seen as subsidiaries of the court and as being guided by the court.

Judicial confirmation of mediation agreements occurring in China requires endorsement by mediation institutions,[4] and China has set relatively stringent admission requirements for mediators. In practice, the system of individual mediation offices is also not individual mediation in the substantive sense, but a mediation organisation established under the name of a people's mediator or a unique name.[5] Individual mediation exists only in individual practices, such as mediation by invited mediators of the people's courts and mediation by lawyers. However, both invited mediation and lawyer mediation are highly dependent on organisations and institutions, and they are actually mediators appointed by or endorsed by organisations or institutions.[6]

Under the Convention, international settlement agreements resulting from individual mediation have the same effect as those resulting from institutional mediation. The provisions of the Convention regarding mediators are different from the existing mediation culture in China, which has been characterised by the intervention of government authority "*for the people*" for decades. On the contrary, commercial mediation is more focused on the autonomy of the parties, and the mediator's function is to "facilitate" the parties' agreement rather than to "conduct" the parties.[7] Consequently, the mediator does not have the power to make decisions in the mediation process. Therefore, the mediator need not be bound by the same mechanisms as an arbitrator or a judge, let alone an institution with a supervisory or sponsorship function.

Although China's domestic regulations do not allow individual mediation, it is also unable to regulate international settlement agreements that apply to the Convention. In other words, parties can apply for enforcement in other signatory states based on international settlement agreements reached in China through individual mediation, and China cannot refuse to enforce international settlement agreements reached in foreign countries through individual mediation. As a result, the question of how to regulate the behaviour of individual mediators is a concern which will need to be addressed by China's ratification of the Convention.

(2) *Verification of disputed facts and application of law by the competent Chinese authorities*

In mediation practice, the finding of disputed facts is no longer significant, and the application of law is more flexible. In China's civil litigation, judicial confirmation of mediation is characterised as an influential way for courts to exercise their jurisdiction. When a settlement agreement of a private nature is transformed into a judicial confirmation document, the court is responsible for its legality.[8]

However, modern commercial mediation reflects not only a "diversion" from the judicial system but also the right to leave the resolution of disputes to the parties, with a deeply-rooted concept of autonomy. As early as the Middle Ages, the spontaneous customary law of merchants emerged along the Mediterranean coast, and with the expansion of foreign trade, traders extended the concept of autonomy from substantive rules to the field of dispute resolution and established merchant courts (known as piepowder courts) in which merchants decided disputes on their own. To some extent, commercial mediation was guided by the spirit of community, with the institutional advantage of not requiring the identification of facts or law, in order to settle disputes amicably and quickly.

Due to the lack of facts in dispute, legal findings, and the basis for liability, international settlement agreements themselves may not provide a direct basis for the judiciary to determine the facts and apply the law, which is why the Convention limits the scope of review by the competent authorities.

As such, the direct enforcement mechanism of the Convention will bring challenges to the Chinese judiciary in dealing with "sham mediation". Sham mediation is a mediation activity in which the parties conspire to harm the rights or interests of third parties through a fictitious substantive dispute, with the intention of using civil procedure to do so. In Chinese practice, the proportion of mediation agreements applying for judicial confirmation is low because debtors are often reluctant to apply for this. However, if the mediation agreement is reached through a sham dispute, the parties are more willing to apply for judicial confirmation.

The Convention's limitation on the scope of review by the competent authority increases the likelihood that enforcement agencies will encounter sham mediations. At the cross-border level, it will also be more difficult for an outsider to file a complaint and for the competent authority to determine the merits of such a complaint. Therefore, preventing judicial enforcement of fraudulent international settlement agreements is also crucial for the successful ratification of the Convention in China.

(3) *Enforcement of international settlement agreements without recognition and reciprocal reservation mechanisms*

The fact that the Convention does not establish the concepts of "seat of mediation" and "country of origin" and does not allow for reciprocal reservations creates at least two risks.

Firstly, no country has the power to revoke an international settlement agreement. International settlement agreements are essentially borderless legal instruments, and they are not subject to domestic law except in enforcement proceedings. Since there is no "nationality" and the international mediation agreement lacks a recognition mechanism, the parties have only the power to deny the enforceability of the international mediation agreement in their own countries, but not the power to revoke or refuse to recognise the international settlement agreement.

Secondly, the enforcement of international mediation agreements is universal. "Universal enforcement" means that parties have an international obligation to enforce international mediation agreements in all countries, whether they are parties or not, as long as the requirements of the Convention are met.

The Convention provides an opportunity for non-parties to "free ride". On the one hand, a party may face "international transfer of cases" and an "enforcement explosion" if it has a high level of cross-border commercial activity and a large number of foreign commercial subjects' assets in the country. On the other hand, "universal enforcement" also exposes the enforcement agencies to legal identification and application challenges. For example, the competent authorities will probably need to track and judge the legal norms related to international commercial mediation in all countries around the world in order to determine whether the international mediation agreement is valid under their governing law. This will obviously make the work of judicial authorities more difficult.[9] In addition, since there are countless mediation institutions and mediators around the world, under the "universal enforcement" system, it may be difficult for the Chinese judiciary to assess the quality of international mediation agreements simply by virtue of the reputation of the mediation institutions and mediators involved. Therefore, how to simplify and facilitate the implementation of international settlement agreements while reducing the burden on the judiciary is also a concern for the ratification of the Convention in China.

III. The Singapore Convention on Mediation and the internationalisation of China's commercial mediation system

There are three main domestic positions on whether China should ratify the Convention. The first is a negative attitude towards ratification. The second is that the Convention should be strictly limited to the scope of international commercial dispute resolution and a "dual-track" system of domestic and international mediation should be implemented.[10] The third advocates for the creation of conditions that would facilitate the ratification and implementation of the Convention.[11]

The reasons for not ratifying the Convention or implementing the "dual-track system" are: (i) the commercial mediation system is incompatible with the long-developed People's Mediation System in China;

(ii) the Convention lacks a reciprocal reservation mechanism, which will lead to inequality of rights and obligations between parties and non-parties; (iii) ratifying the Convention will make China assume more enforcement obligations and put pressure on the judiciary; and (iv) the Convention does not contain provisions on the qualification of mediators, which runs the risk of fraudulent mediation.

However, at the international level, China has already signed the Convention, and even if it has not yet ratified it, under Article 18 of the Vienna Convention on the Law of Treaties, China should treat its obligations under the Convention in good faith and should not maliciously undermine the object and purpose of the Convention. Therefore, China should actively explore the necessary rule of law reforms and work to create the conditions for ratification of the Convention. From the international political point of view, ratifying the Convention is of great significance, as it fully demonstrates to the world the Chinese government's firm position of supporting multilateralism, defending the international rule of law, operating a market economy, and respecting commercial autonomy.

At the domestic level, the benefits of ratifying and implementing the Convention generally outweigh the disadvantages of building China's commercial rule of law. Specifically, the ratification and implementation of the Convention will help improve China's commercial legal system. In 2020, China's total import and export value of trade in goods reached RMB 32.16 trillion. In 2019, more than 27,500 domestic investors set up 4.4 million outward foreign direct investment enterprises in 188 countries (regions) worldwide.[12]

However, compared to China's huge overseas economic interests, China's commercial dispute resolution concepts and rules are outdated and increasingly endanger the security of Chinese enterprises' interests overseas. Statistics have shown that 90% of Chinese disputes which occur abroad are settled outside China, and over 90% of these arbitration cases are unsuccessful. This is related to the lack of standardised, modern, and systematic commercial dispute resolution norms.

The Convention's pursuit of commercial autonomy, integrity, and professional mediation aligns with China's goal of developing a commercial dispute resolution mechanism. Moreover, ratifying the Convention is an inevitable way to safeguard its overseas interests by applying rule of law thinking and methods. In turn, the implementation of the Convention can also promote the integrity, rule of law, and modernisation of China's social governance, and further promote the construction of a business environment underpinned by rule of law.

The Convention specifies the conditions for the enforcement of international settlement agreements, but the specific enforcement rules are determined by domestic law. In this regard, China could build a dovetailing domestic enforcement mechanism, and after clarifying the independent remedial function of international settlement agreements and the review and supervisory power of the judiciary, motivate the parties to express their intention to apply the Convention, and build a comprehensive code for mediators.

China could also approach ratifying the Convention as an opportunity to promote the gradual growth of its domestic commercial mediation sector and bring it in line with international markets. In the process, this would nurture a team of commercial mediators and mediation service providers with a global reputation and a number of commercial mediation institutions with international influence. In turn, the modernisation of the commercial mediation industry may encourage Chinese companies to use their own mediators more confidently to resolve foreign-related disputes, and may make foreign companies more willing to accept China's mediation services and apply for enforcement abroad.

IV. Conclusion

As of writing, only 11 countries have ratified the Convention since it came into force. Many signatories still remain on the sidelines because of the Convention's "universal enforcement" mechanism. At present, the prospect of the US returning to multilateralism is unclear, and the EU and Japan have not yet signed the Convention, but the US, UK, Germany, France, and the Netherlands are competing fiercely for the international commercial dispute resolution services market. The core of this market competition lies in competition between systems. China will need to continue to observe other countries' positions on the Convention, especially those with which it has important economic and trade relations, and gradually improve its domestic legal system of international commercial mediation, in order to create favourable conditions for the ratification of the Convention and enable it to decide whether to do so in a timely manner.

https://doi.org/10.1142/9789811285257_bmatter

Endnotes

Chapter 1 Operationalising Article 5(1)(e) of the Singapore Convention on Mediation

1. Convention on the Recognition and Enforcement of Foreign Arbitral Awards [1958] 330 UNTS 3 ("the New York Convention").
2. G.A. Res. 73/198, U.N. Doc. A/Res/73/198, annex, United Nations Convention on International Settlement Agreements Resulting from Mediation (11 January 2019) ("the Singapore Convention on Mediation").
3. As of 5 June 2023.
4. Singapore International Dispute Resolution Academy, *A Handbook on the Singapore Convention on Mediation* (2020) at 18.
5. See Article V of the New York Convention.
6. Michel Kallipetis, "Singapore Convention Defences Based on Mediator's Misconduct: Articles 5.1(e) & (f)" (2019) 20 *Cardozo Journal of Conflict Resolution* 1197 at 1200.
7. Ibid at 1201.
8. Ibid.
9. UNCITRAL, Report of Working Group II (Dispute Settlement) on the work of its sixty-sixth session, 6–10 February 2017 UN Doc. A/CN.9/901 (2017) ("Report of Working Group II") at 74.
10. Report of Working Group II, see note 8 at 75.
11. Ibid.
12. Report of Working Group II, see note 8 at 79.
13. Ibid.
14. See Article 2(3) of the Singapore Convention on Mediation.
15. Omer Shapira, "A Critical Assessment of the Model Standards of Conduct for Mediators" (2005) 100:1 *Marquette Law Review* 81 at 83.
16. American Arbitration Association, *Model Standards of Conduct for Mediators* (2005), Standard 1(A).
17. *Kallipetis*, see note 6 at 1200.

18. Ibid.
19. Ibid.
20. Nancy A. Welsh, "The Thinning Vision of Self-Determination in Court-Connected Mediation: The Inevitable Price of Institutionalization?" (2001) 6 *Harvard Negotiation Law Review* 1 at 79.
21. Penny Brooker, *Mediation Law: Journey through Institutionalism to Juridification* (Routledge, 2013) at 103.
22. *Kallipetis*, see note 6 at 1198.
23. For instance, the Singapore courts in *Surindar Singh s/o Jaswant Singh v Sita Jaswant Kaur* [2014] 3 SLR 1284 (CA) at [60]; *Gay Choon Ing* [2009] 2 SLR(R) 332 (CA) at [54] and [56]; and *Lee Kuan Yew v Chee Soon Juan* [2003] 3 SLR(R) 8 (HC) at [25].
24. *Welsh*, see note 19 at 83.
25. Ibid.
26. Ibid.
27. *Welsh*, see note 19 at 84.
28. Report of Working Group II, see note 8 at 82.
29. *Surindar Singh s/o Jaswant Singh v Sita Jaswant Kaur* [2014] SGCA 37; [2014] 3 SLR 1284 ("*Surindar Singh*").
30. Dorcas Quek Anderson, "Litigating Over Mediation — How Should the Courts Enforce Mediated Settlement Agreements?" (2015) *Singapore Journal of Legal Studies* 105 at 127; *Surindar Singh* at [25].
31. *Kallipetis,* see note 6 at 1207.
32. *Kallipetis,* see note 6 at 1203.
33. See Section 9(3)(a) of the Mediation Act 2017.
34. *Unilever Plc v The Procter & Gamble Co* [2000] 1 WLR 2536 (CA) ("*Unilever*").
35. Penny Brooker, "Judging Unreasonable Litigation Behavior at the Interface of Mediation in the English Jurisdiction" (2010) 2:3 *Journal of Legal Affairs and Dispute Resolution in Engineering and Construction* 155.
36. *Unilever* at [23].
37. Ibid.
38. *Kallipetis*, see note 6 at 1205; citing *Forster v Friedland CA* (Civil Division), Transcript No. 205 of 1993 (Eng. & Wales).
39. *Farm Assist Ltd v Secretary of State for the Environment, Food and Rural Affairs (DEFRA) (No. 2)* [2009] EWHC 1102 (TCC) (May 19, 2009) ("*Farm Assist*").
40. *Farm Assist* at [51].

41. *Brooker*, see note 35 at 155; citing Hamish Lal, "Commercial exploitation in construction contracts: the role of economic duress and unjust enrichment" (2005) 21:8 *Construction Law Journal* 590 at 591.
42. *Quek Anderson*, see note 29 at 128; citing Ellen E. Deason. "Enforcing Mediated Settlement Agreement: Contract Law Collides with Confidentiality" (2001–2002) 5 *UC Davis Law Review* 33 at 89.
43. Ibid.
44. *Kallipetis*, see note 6 at 1198.
45. Section 6(b) of the US Uniform Mediation Act.
46. Ibid.
47. *Quek Anderson,* see note 29 at 128.
48. *Quek Anderson*, see note 29 at 118; citing James J. Alfini & Catherine McCabe "Mediating in the Shadow of the Courts: A Survey of the Emerging Case Law" (2001–2002) 54 *Arkansas Law Review* 171 at 206.
49. *Quek Anderson,* see note 29 at 128.
50. For instance, in *AB v CD Limited* [2013] EWHC 1376 (TCC) at [35], the judge directed that the judgement deciding whether a binding settlement agreement was reached be appropriately anonymised, due to the need for confidentiality about the terms of the settlement.
51. For instance, in *Hall v Pertemps Group Ltd* [2005] ADR.L.R. 11/01 at [14], Mr Justice Lewison opined that "the more relevant to the underlying dispute the impropriety is the more likely they are to be covered by the without prejudice protection".
52. *Quek Anderson,* see note 29 at 128.
53. Report of Working Group II, see note 8 at 87.
54. *Kallipetis*, see note 6 at 1201.
55. Report of Working Group II, see note 8 at 80.
56. Nadja Alexander and Shouyu Chong, "Article 5(1)(e)–(f) Mediator Conduct-Related Grounds for Refusal" in Nadja Alexander and Shouyu Chong (eds.), *The Singapore Convention on Mediation: A Commentary* (Kluwer Law International, 2019).
57. Model Standards of Conduct for Mediators, Standard II.
58. Singapore International Mediation Institute, Code of Professional Conduct for SIMI Mediators, Standard 4.1.
59. *Alexander and Chong*, see note 56 at 5.71.
60. For a view advocating that mediators owe broader duties to the progression of mediation and to the public, see *Shapira*, note 14 at 96 et seq.
61. *Kallipetis*, see note 6 at 1200.

62. Report of Working Group II, see note 8 at 86.
63. *Kallipetis*, see note 6 at 1198.
64. James Coben, "Evaluating the Singapore Convention Through a U.S.-Centric Litigation Lens: Lessons Learned from Nearly Two Decades of Mediation Disputes in American Federal and State Courts" (2019) 20 *Cardozo Journal of Conflict Resolution* 106.
65. *Quek Anderson*, see note 29 at 118.

Chapter 2 The Hesitation of the European Union in Adopting the Singapore Convention on Mediation: Perspectives from International Relations Theory

1. See United Nations Commission on International Trade Law (UNCITRAL), "Status: United Nations Convention on International Settlement Agreements Resulting from Mediation' <https://uncitral.un.org/en/texts/mediation/conventions/international_settlement_agreements/status> (accessed 24 September 2023).
2. Sherina Petit, "The Singapore Convention on Mediation: A New Enforcement Regime", *Norton Rose Fulbright* (August 2019) <https://www.nortonrosefulbright.com/en/knowledge/publications/376106c1/the-singapore-convention-on-mediation--a-new-enforcement-regime> (accessed 31 May 2022).
3. United Nations Convention on International Settlement Agreements Resulting from Mediation (adopted 20 December 2018, entered into force 12 September 2020) 22 UNTS 4.
4. Morrison Foerster, 'Singapore Convention on Mediation Enters into Force' (12 September 2020) <https://www.mofo.com/resources/insights/200912-singapore-convention-on-mediation-enters-into-force.html> (accessed 31 May 2022).
5. Ministry of Law Singapore, "Opening Address by Mr K Shanmugam, Minister for Home Affairs and Minister for Law, for SIAC India Summit 2019 Day One: Investor-State Dispute Settlement" (30 August 2019) <https://www.mlaw.gov.sg/news/speeches/opening-address-by-minister-shanmugam-for-siac-investment-arbitration-conference> (accessed 31 May 2022).
6. Henneke Brink, "The Singapore Convention on Mediation — Where's Europe?", *Mediate.com* (26 March 2021) <https://www.mediate.com/articles/brink-singapore-europe.cfm> (accessed 31 May 2022).

7. Haris Meidanis, "Singapore Convention Series: A Plea for the Adoption of the Singapore Mediation Convention by the EU", *Kluwer Mediation Blog* (20 March 2019) <http://mediationblog.kluwerarbitration.com/2019/03/20/singapore-convention-series-a-plea-for-the-adoption-of-the-singapore-mediation-convention-by-the-eu/> (accessed 31 May 2022).
8. Council Directive 2008/52/EC of 21 May 2008 on certain aspects of mediation in civil and commercial matters [2008] OJ L 136/3, Preamble at [7], [10].
9. *Brink,* see note 6.
10. Javier Fernández-Samaniego, "The Effects of Cross-Border Disputes One Year after the Entry Into Force of the Singapore Mediation Convention" (2022) 40(1) *Alternatives to the High Cost of Litigation* 3 at 4.
11. James G. March and Johan P. Olsen, "The Institutional Dynamics of International Political Orders" (1998) 52(4) *International Organization* 943 at 948.
12. Scott Burchill, "Liberalism" in Scott Burchill and Andrew Linklater (eds.), *Theories of International Relations* (Houndmills: Palgrave, 5th Edition, 2013) at 67–68.
13. Thomas Risse, "Social Constructivism and European Integration" in Antje Wiener and Thomas Diez (eds.), *European Integration Theory* (Oxford University Press, 2nd Edition, 2009) at 147.
14. *March and Olsen*, see note 11 at 949.
15. *Burchill*, see note 12 at 66.
16. European Commission, "The European Union: What it is and what it does" (1 February 2020) <https://op.europa.eu/en/publication-detail/-/publication/ac0a88a6-4369-11ea-b81b-01aa75ed71a1> (accessed 31 May 2022).
17. *Burchill*, see note 12 at 67–68.
18. European Union, "Regulations, Directives and other acts" (29 September 2020) <https://europa.eu/european-union/law/legal-acts_en> (accessed 31 May 2022).
19. *March and Olsen*, see note 11 at 951.
20. Christian Reus-Smit, "Constructivism" in Scott Burchill and Andrew Linklater (eds.), *Theories of International Relations* (Houndmills: Palgrave, 5th Edition, 2013) 224–226.
21. *Risse,* see note 13 at 148.
22. *March and Olsen*, see note 11 at 952.
23. *Risse,* see note 13 at 148 and 153–154.
24. Steven E. Lobell, "Structural Realism/Offensive and Defensive Realism", *Oxford Research Encyclopedia of International Studies* (12 December 2017)

<https://oxfordre.com/internationalstudies/view/10.1093/acrefore/9780190846626.001.0001/acrefore-9780190846626-e-304> (accessed 31 May 2022).

25. Kenneth Waltz, *Theory of International Politics* (Addison-Wesley Publishing Company, 1979) at 102–126.
26. Charles L. Glaser, "Realists as Optimists: Cooperation as Self-Help" (1994–95) 19(3) *International Security* 50 at 68–70.
27. The World Bank, "GDP (current US$) — European Union'" <https://data.worldbank.org/indicator/NY.GDP.MKTP.CD?locations=EU> (accessed 31 May 2022).
28. European Commission, "The three largest global players for international trade" (30 September 2021) <https://ec.europa.eu/eurostat/statistics-explained/index.php?title=International_trade_in_goods#The_three_largest_global_players_for_international_trade:_EU.2C_China_and_the_USA> (accessed 31 May 2022).
29. *Meidanis*, see note 7.

Chapter 3 Keeping Confidentiality or Pursuing Transparency: The Dilemma of Transparency in Investor-State Mediation Mechanism

1. Fan Xiaoyu (Ph.D., Wuhan University Institute of International Law, with Concentration in International Investment Law and International Dispute Resolution) is a Legal Researcher of Wuhan University Institute of International Law and Wuhan University Center of Oversea Investment Law. The full version of this article was originally published in the *Groningen Journal of International Law* (2022) 9(2).
2. This article makes no distinction between conciliation and mediation. There is some controversy in the academic world concerning whether mediation and conciliation are identical. Some scholars believe that the differences between the two terms reflect conceptual differences; see Gabriele Ruscala, "Latest Developments in Conciliation and Mediation in Investor-State Disputes" (2019) 16(63) *Revista Brasileira de Arbitragem* 98. Others believe that there is no clear boundary between conciliation and mediation and that they are interchangeable; see Michael E Schneider, '"Investment Disputes: Moving Beyond Arbitration" in Laurence Boisson de Chazournes, Marcelo G Kohen and Jorge E Viñuales (eds.), *Diplomatic and Judicial Means of Dispute Settlement* (Brill, 2012) at 119. Recent treaties, such as the United

Nations Convention on International Settlement Agreements Resulting from Mediation (adopted on 20 December 2018, entered into force 12 September 2020) CN.154.2019.TREATIES-XXII.4 <https://uncitral.un.org/en/texts/mediation/conventions/international_settlement_agreements> (accessed April 30 2021) and the UNCITRAL Model Law on International Commercial Mediation and International Settlement Agreements Resulting from Mediation (adopted in 2018, amending the Model Law on International Commercial Conciliation 2002) <https://uncitral.un.org/en/texts/mediation/modellaw/commercial_conciliation> (accessed 30 April 2021)) also use the term "mediation", with the understanding that the terms "conciliation" and "mediation" are interchangeable. Given these recent trends in international mediation rules, this article uses the term "mediation" to refer to both mediation and conciliation and holds the view that the two terms can be used interchangeably, except in specific contexts where they denote two different procedures, such as under the International Centre for Settlement of Investment Disputes (ICSID). The seven key differences between ICSID conciliation and ICSID mediation can be found in ICSID, "Background Paper on Investment Mediation" (July 2021) <https://icsid.worldbank.org/sites/default/files/publications/Background_Paper_on_Investment_Mediation_Oct.2021.pdf> (accessed 28 January 2022).

3. According to the ICSID, of the 728 cases registered since 1982, only 12 were conciliation cases, 10 (1.4%) of which were under the ICSID Convention, Regulations and Rules (entered into force 14 October 1966) and 2 (0.3%) were under the ICSID Conciliation (Additional Facility) Rules. See ICSID, "Caseload: Statistics 2019" 2019 (2) <https://icsid.worldbank.org/sites/default/files/publications/Caseload%20Statistics/en/The%20ICSID%20Caseload%20Statistics%20%282019-2%20Edition%29%20ENG.pdf> (accessed 30 April 2021).
4. Seraphina Chew, Lucy Reed, and J Christopher Thomas, "Report: Survey on Obstacles to Settlement of Investor-State Disputes" (2018) NUS Centre for International Law Research Paper 18/01 and NUS Law Working Paper 2018/022.
5. Shahla F Ali and Odysseas G Repousis, "Investor–State Mediation and the Rise of Transparency in International Investment Law: Opportunity or Threat" (2016) 45(2) *Denver Journal of International Law & Policy* 225.
6. Jack J Coe Jr, "Should Mediation of Investment Disputes Be Encouraged, and, If So, by Whom and How?" in Arthur W Rovine (ed.), *Contemporary Issues in International Arbitration and Mediation: The Fordham Papers 2009* (Brill, 2010) at 349.

7. Maria Beatrice Deli, "Transparency in the Arbitral Procedure" in Andrea Gattini, Attila Tanzi, and Filippo Fontanelli (eds.), *General Principles of Law and International Investment Arbitration* (Brill, 2018) at 56.
8. *Coe*, see note 6 at 349.
9. Ana Ubilava and Luke R Nottage, "ICSID's New Mediation Rules: A Small but Positive Step Forward" (2018) ICSID World Bank, Submission to ICSID on ICSID Rules and Regulations Amendment Process 3 <https://icsid.worldbank.org/sites/default/files/amendments/public-input/Ubilava_Notage_10.17.2018.pdf> (accessed 30 April 2021).
10. Catharine Titi, "Mediation and the Settlement of International Investment Disputes: Between Utopia and Realism" in Catharine Titi and Katia Fach Gómez (eds.), *Mediation in International Commercial and Investment Disputes* (Oxford University Press, 2019) at 35.
11. Susan D Franck and Anna Joubin-Bret (eds.), (2010). "Investor-State Disputes: Prevention and Alternatives to Arbitration II" in Proceedings of the Washington and Lee University and UNCTAD Joint Symposium on International Investment and Alternative Dispute Resolution, (2010) at 11.
12. Daniel Barstow Magraw and Niranjali Manel Amerasinghe, "Transparency and Public Participation in Investor–State Arbitration" (2009) 15 *ILSA Journal of International & Comparative Law* 337 at 351.
13. Ximena Bustamante, "Investor–State Mediation: Reflections on its Feasibility from a Process Perspective" in Todd Weiler and Freya Baetens (eds.), *New Directions in International Economic Law* (Brill, 2011) at 275 and 297.
14. The 1967 Freedom of Information Act 5 USC § 552 (FOIA) imposes a statutory obligation on US federal government agencies to comply with requests for information contained in government records, subject to specific, enumerated exceptions.
15. Daniel Barstow Magraw, Sofia Plagakis and Jessica Schifano, "Ways and Means of Citizens' Participation in Trade and Investment Dispute Settlement Procedures", Society of International Economic Law (SIEL) Inaugural Conference paper (2008) at 101 <http://dx.doi.org/10.2139/ssrn.1159770> (accessed 30 April 2021).
16. Sarah J K Rauber, "Investor–State Mediation in International Investment Dispute Settlement — a Critical, Integral Multi- and Transdisciplinary Analysis: Analysis & Development of Policy Implications and Practical Guidelines, with a Particular Focus on De-Biasing the Mediation Process" (22 August 2016) <http://dx.doi.org/10.2139/ssrn.3115955> (accessed 30 April 2021).

17. Steffen Hindelang, "Study on Investor–State Dispute Settlement (ISDS) and Alternatives to Dispute Resolution in International Investment Law" (2016) 13(1) *Transnational Dispute Management* 1 at 97.
18. For examples of the practice of investment arbitration, see, *inter alia, Methanex v United States, The Glamis Gold Ltd v United States, Aguas Argentinas et al. v Argentina Republic, Biwater v Tanzania, Metalclad v Mexico.*
19. See the UNCITRAL Rules on Transparency in Treaty-based Investor–State Arbitration; ICSID Arbitration Rules of Proposals For Amendment Of The ICSID Rules (21 March 2022).
20. See International Bar Association Council, IBA Rules for Investor-State Mediation Article 10(1) (adopted 4 October 2012) <https://icsid.worldbank.org/sites/default/files/IBA%20Rules%20for%20Investor-State%20Mediation%20(Approved%20by%20IBA%20Council%204%20Oct%202012)_0.pdf> (accessed 30 April 2021); the EU-Canada Comprehensive Economic and Trade Agreement (CETA) 'Annex 29-C: Rules of Procedure for Mediation' at Article 6(1) (signed 30 October 2016, not entered into force); the Energy Charter Secretar, Decision of the Energy Charter Conference: the Guide on Investment Mediation (19 July 2016) CCDEC12 INV <https://www.energycharter.org/fileadmin/DocumentsMedia/CCDECS/2016/CCDEC201612.pdf> (accessed 30 April 2020), and the Asia-Pacific Regional Mediation Organization, Draft "Rules of Procedure for Mediation Conducted Under the Asia-Pacific Regional Mediation Organization" at Article 15 <https://drive.google.com/file/d/1_N8pNxaY_Wuo7F-jpVAup_H7Pyfxe4UG/view> (accessed 30 April 2021).
21. See the IBA Rules for Investor-State Mediation, note 20 at Article 10(1).
22. See the ICSID Proposed Regulations and Rules for ICSID Mediation Proceedings at Rule 10(1), available at <https://icsid.worldbank.org/sites/default/files/publications/rule_amendment_proposals_mediation.pdf> (accessed 29 January 2022). Similar regulations can be found in Article 6(1) of the EU-Canada Comprehensive Economic and Trade Agreement (CETA) 'Annex 29-C-Rules of Procedure for Mediation'; the IBA Rules for Investor-State Mediation at note 20, Article 10(2); and the ARMO at note 20, Article 15.
23. See CETA Annex 29-C — Rules of Procedure for Mediation, note 22 at Article 6(4); ARMO, note 20 at Article 15(3); and the Proposed Regulations And Rules For ICSID Mediation Proceedings, note 20 at Rule 11.

24. Lawrence R Freedman and Michael L Prigoff, "Confidentiality in Mediation: The Need for Protection" (1986) 2 *Ohio State Journal on Dispute Resolution* 37.
25. Peter D Cameron and Abba Kolo, "Mediating International Energy Disputes" in Catharine Titi and Katia Fach Gómez (eds.), *Mediation in International Commercial and Investment Disputes* (Oxford University Press, 2019) at 237.
26. *Titi*, see note 10 at 35.
27. *Freedman and Prigoff,* see note 24 at 37.
28. Ibid.
29. Ibid.
30. Thomas W Walde, "Proactive Mediation of International Business and Investment Disputes Involving Long-Term Contracts: From Zero-Sum Litigation to Efficient Dispute Management" (2004) 5 *Business Law International* 99–101.
31. Jack J Coe, "Towards a Complementary Use of Conciliation in Investor–State Disputes — A Preliminary Sketch" (2005) 12 *UC Davis Journal of International Law* 7 at 17.
32. Nancy A Welsh and Andrea K Schneider, "The Thoughtful Integration of Mediation into Bilateral Investment Treaty Arbitration" (2013) 18 *Harvard Negotiation Law Review* 71 at 77.
33. Chester Brown and Phoebe Winch, "The Confidentiality and Transparency Debate in Commercial and Investment" in Catharine Titi and Katia Fach Gómez (eds.), *Mediation in International Commercial and Investment Disputes* (Oxford University Press, 2019) at 324.
34. *Titi,* see note 10 at 36; Edna Sussman, "The Advantages of Mediation and the Special Challenges to its Utilization in Investor–State Disputes" (2010) 7 *Revista Brasileira de Arbitragem* 6.
35. *Titi,* see note 10 at 36.
36. *Coe,* see note 6 at 349.
37. *Ubilava and Nottage*, see note 9 at 3.
38. Emilie M Hafner-Burton, Sergio Puig and David G Victor, 'Against Secrecy: The Social Cost of International Dispute Settlement" (2017) 45 *Yale Journal of International Law* 2.
39. Timothy Schnabel, "The Singapore Convention on Mediation: A Framework for the Cross-Border Recognition and Enforcement of Mediated Settlements" (2019) 19 *Pepperdine Dispute Resolution Law Journal* 1.
40. *Sussman*, see note 34 at 6.

41. See the Decision of the Energy Charter Conference: the Guide on Investment Mediation, 10.C; the IBA Rules for Investor-State Mediation, note 20 at Article 10 and ARMO, note 20 at Article 15(4).
42. See the Proposed Regulations And Rules For ICSID Mediation Proceedings (20 January 2022), Rule 10(1); CETA 'Annex 29-C — Rules of Procedure for Mediation' at note 22 at Article 6(1); the IBA Rules for Investor-State Mediation at note 20 at Article 10(2); and ARMO at note 20 at Article 15(3).
43. See the IBA Rules for Investor-State Mediation, note 20 at Article 10.3(a); CETA Annex 29-C — Rules of Procedure for Mediation, note 22 at Article 6(1); the EU-Vietnam Agreement Annex 9: Mediation Mechanism at Article 7; and the Decision of the Energy Charter Conference: the Guide on Investment Mediation, 10.C.
44. See the IBA Rules for Investor-State Mediation, note 20 at Article 10.3(b) and the Decision of the Energy Charter Conference: the Guide on Investment Mediation, 10.C.
45. See CETA Annex 29-C — Rules of Procedure for Mediation, note 22 at Article 7(3).
46. See ICSID, Proposed Regulations and Rules for ICSID Mediation Proceedings at 10(1).
47. See the IBA Rules for Investor-State Mediation, note 20 at Article 10.3.

Chapter 4 Healing the Healer: It is Okay to Not Be Okay

1. Katie Reed, "What is Self Care and Why is It Important To Your Health?"<https://www.katiereed.com/what-is-self-care-and-why-is-it-important-to-your-health/> (26 February 2021) (accessed 10 April 2022).
2. Linda Lazarus, "Mediation as a Hearing Art: A Conversation with Daniel Benor, M.D." (September 2005) <https://www.mediate.com/articles/lazarusL6.cfm> (accessed 19 March 2022). See also Zena D. Zumeta, "Spirituality and mediation" (1993) 11 *Mediation Quarterly* 25 at 29–30. The author argues that "[when] people say that mediation is healing, they generally mean that the rupture between them is healed to one extent or another, and they experience more connectedness than they did before."
3. The story of the eighteenth camel is a fable where the addition of the eighteenth camel allowed for a mathematically-sound distribution of the existing seventeen camels. This fable's takeaway is that mediators should value-add as the eighteenth camel and help the parties reach a solution which may not be visible at first glance. See, e.g., the mediation1st website <https://www.

mediation1st.co.uk/?p=the.story.of.the.mediator.and.the.17.camels> (accessed 19 March 2022).

4. Michael Jacobs, “Mediator Burnout” (August 2012) <https://www.mediate.com/articles/JacobsM8.cfm> (accessed 28 March 2022).
5. Susan S. Raines, Sunil Kumar Pokhrel and Jean Poitras, “Mediation as a Profession: Challenges that Professional Mediators Face” (2013) 31 *Conflict Resolution Quarterly* 79 at 80.
6. Charles R. Figley, “Compassion fatigue: psychotherapists’ chronic lack of self-care” (2002) *Journal of Clinical Psychology* 58:1433–144, at 1436, citing Ayala Pines and Elliot Aronson, *Career burnout: Causes and cures* (New York: The Free Press, 1988) at 9.
7. Christina Maslach, Wilmar B. Schaufeli and Michael P. Leiter, “Job Burnout” (2001) *Annual Review of Psychology* 52: 397–422 at 403.
8. Lee Norton, Jennifer Johnson and George Woods, “Burnout and Compassion Fatigue: What Lawyers Need to Know” (2016) 84 *University of Missouri-Kansas City Law Review* 987 at 988.
9. See, e.g., Caroline Harmon-Darrow and Yanfeng Xu, “Retaining volunteer mediators: Comparing predictors of burnout” (2018) 35 *Conflict Resolution Quarterly* 367.
10. Lydia Nussbaum, “Mediator Burnout” (2019) 34 *Ohio State Journal on Dispute Resolution* 171 at 191.
11. See, e.g., the State Courts of Singapore Code of Ethics and Basic Principles on Court Mediation, Clause 3.2 on impartiality and neutrality <https://www.judiciary.gov.sg/docs/default-source/civil-docs/mediation_code_of_cthics_state_courts.pdf> (accessed 2 April 2022).
12. *Nussbaum,* see note 10 at 193.
13. R3 Resolutions website, “Vicarious trauma — 3 observations from the mediator’s chair” (25 November 2020) <https://r3resolutions.com.au/vicarious-trauma-3-observations-from-the-mediators-chair/> (accessed 28 March 2022).
14. *Nussbaum,* see note 10 at 193.
15. Ibid at 192.
16. Ibid at 194.
17. Ibid.
18. Wayne D. Brazil, “Thoughts about Spiritual Fatigue: Sustaining Our Energy by Staying Centered” (2008) 2 Journal of Dispute Resolution 411 at 417–421.
19. Perhaps this essay’s introduction may also be guilty of portraying mediation and mediators in an overly positive light by analogising mediators to healers.

20. Charlie Irvine, "The 'F-word' for mediators — failure" Kluwer Mediation Blog (13 August 2012) <http://mediationblog.kluwerarbitration.com/2012/08/13/the-f-word-for-mediators-failure/> (accessed 2 April 2022).
21. See, e.g., the Singapore Mediation Centre website <https://www.mediation.com.sg/about-us/testimonials/> (accessed 2 April 2022). The Singapore Mediation Centre has a settlement rate of "approximately 70%, with more than 90% of the settled disputes resolved within a day".
22. Mary Elizabeth Lund, "A focus on emotion in mediation training" (2000) 38 *Family & Conciliation Courts Review* 62 at 67.
23. See, e.g., Isabelle Liew and John Elijah Gan, "Woman who suffered noise from neighbour upstairs for three years lost sleep, job" *The Straits Times* (8 March 2022) <https://www.straitstimes.com/singapore/housing/woman-who-suffered-noise-from-upstairs-neighbour-for-three-years-lost-sleep-job> (accessed 2 April 2022).
24. *Lund*, see note 22.
25. *Maslach, Schaufeli and Leiter,* see note 7 at 411. This hypothesis has received mixed empirical support, with about equal number of studies finding the hypothesised correlation, while the rest do not.
26. *Norton, Johnson and Woods*, see note 8 at 988, citing Dennis Portnoy, "Burnout and Compassion Fatigue: Watch for the Signs" (2011) *Health Progress* 92(4) 46–50 at 47.
27. Ibid, citing note 6. Jonathan W. Reitman, "Mediator Fatigue: The Traumatic Effect of What We Hear" (November 2007) <https://www.mediate.com/articles/reitmanJ5.cfm> (accessed 2 April 2022). The author argues that "[e]viction cases, property issues, victim-offender mediations, labor-management situations and even commercial disputes — all of these may provoke traumatic experiences for the parties. If we're doing our job and remaining 'present,' we mediators often feel deep feelings of empathy and sorrow for the parties' suffering."
28. I. Lisa McCann and Laurie Anne Pearlman, "Vicarious traumatization: A framework for understanding the psychological effects of working with victims" (1990) *Journal of Traumatic Stress* 3 131–149 at 144. See also TEND Academy website <https://www.tendacademy.ca/what-is-compassion-fatigue/> (accessed 2 April 2022).
29. Kylie Nomchong, "Vicarious trauma in the legal profession" (2017) 79 *New South Wales Bar Association News* 35. While this article focused on explaining how lawyers experience vicarious trauma, its findings may be relevant to mediators as well, especially those dealing with violent or traumatic disputes.

30. Ann M. Ordway, Ruth Ouzts Moore, Arielle F. Casasnovas and Nancy R. Asplund, "Understanding Vicarious Trauma, Burnout, and Compassion Fatigue in High-Conflict Divorce" (2020) *The Family Journal: Counseling and Therapy for Couples and Families* 28(2) 187–193 at 189–190.
31. See e.g., *Maslach, Schaufeli and Leiter,* note 7 at 406.
32. *Nussbaum,* see note 10 at 201–208.
33. Ibid at 202. The author argues that mediators are guardians of mediation quality through informal and formal norms. See also at 210 where the author argues that mediators add value to legal negotiations by providing structure to negotiations.
34. In Singapore, pre-mediation conferences are not conducted for every case. For example, for mediations at the Community Mediation Centre, the mediators will meet the parties for the first time during the mediation session, although they would have read the case brief prior to the start of the session. See e.g. Community Mediation Centre website, "The Mediation Process" <https://cmc.mlaw.gov.sg/apply-for-mediation/the-mediation-process/> (accessed 2 April 2022).
35. Cornelia Brinkmann, "Steps for Peace, Working Manual for Peace building and Conflict Management" (December 2006) <http://www.peace-building.org/pdf/Brinkmann-for-peace.pdf> at 50 (accessed 2 April 2022).
36. Elizabeth E. Badar, "The Psychology and Neurobiology of Mediation" (2016) 17(2) *Cardozo Journal of Conflict Resolution* 363 at 363.
37. Daniel Bowling and David Hoffman, "Bringing Peace into the Room: The Personal Qualities of the Mediator and Their Impact on the Mediation" (2000) 16 *Negotiation Journal* 5 at 23.
38. *Nussbaum,* see note 10 at 211–212.
39. Example of reframing include reframing from the past to the future, positions to interests, the negative to the positive, toxic to neutral language, one-side to mutual interests, etc.
40. *Nussbaum,* see note 10 at 208–209.
41. Ibid at 208.
42. Ibid at 210.
43. Ibid at 209.
44. Douglas E. Noll, "Meditation, then mediation" (2007) *Dispute Resolution Magazine* 14(1) 37.
45. Daniel Weitz, "The Brains behind mediation: reflections on neuroscience, conflict resolution and decision-making" (2011) 12 *Cardozo Journal of Conflict Resolution* 471 at 484.

46. *Ordway, Moore, Casasnovas and Asplund*, see note 30 at 191.
47. Ibid.
48. Organisations and groups have been increasingly raising awareness about the issue of mediator burnout and coping mechanisms. See, e.g., Society of Mediation Professionals (Singapore) LinkedIn post (March 2022) <https://www.linkedin.com/posts/smp-sg_mediators-and-mental-health-activity-6905413270975447040-r9dq/> (accessed 2 April 2022). See also Lawyers & Mediators YouTube video, "The Mind and Body in Conflict Resolution With Julia Morelli" (30 August 2021) <https://www.youtube.com/watch?v=jgcg6h6djjg> (accessed 2 April 2022).
49. Barry Nobel, "Meditation and Mediation" (2005) 43(2) *Family Court Review* 295 at 299. While meditation is often associated with religions such as Buddhism, "meditation practice itself need not be confined to religious establishments or private altars".
50. *Ordway, Moore, Casasnovas and Asplund,* see note 30 at 191.
51. Kenneth Cloke, "Mediation and Meditation: The Deeper Middle Way" (March 2009) <https://www.mediate.com/articles/cloke10.cfm> (accessed 2 April 2022).
52. *Ordway, Moore, Casasnovas and Asplund*, see note 30 at 192.
53. Richard L. Harrison and Marvin J. Westwood, "Preventing vicarious traumatization of mental health therapists: identifying protective practices" (2009) *Psychotherapy* 46(2) 203–219 at 208.
54. See e.g., Ministry of Law Singapore website, "Getting to the Heart of Community Conflicts" (18 March 2022) <https://insight.mlaw.gov.sg/articles/our-people/2022-03-18-getting-to-the-heart-of-community-conflicts> (accessed 2 April 2022). The Singapore Community Mediation Centre has a mentoring programme where it usually pairs a less experienced mediator with a more experienced colleague during a session so the junior mediators can learn from their more senior counterparts.
55. See e.g., Keryn Foley, "To Co-Mediate or Not to Co-Mediate — That Is the Question" (2017) 29 *Bond Law Review* 95. The author discusses the pros and cons of co-mediation.
56. Eric R. Galton, *Ripples from Peace Lake: Essays for Mediators and Peacemakers* (Trafford, 2004) at 163.
57. See, e.g., Grace Yeoh, "Back-to-back crises, days that end at 4am: Why some social workers in Singapore are burning out" *Channel NewsAsia* (17 April 2022) <https://www.channelnewsasia.com/singapore/social-workers-burnout-job-hours-passion-2553816> (accessed 17 April 2022). One social worker

who was interviewed shared that "placing too much emphasis on passion as a driving force in caregiving sectors can be 'harmful.'" Similarly, this may be relevant to mediators.

Chapter 5 Navigating Two Different Truths in Family Mediation: One Size Will Not Fit All

1. Daniel Kahneman, *Thinking, Fast and Slow* (Macmillan, 2011).
2. Brianna Wiest, *101 Essays That Will Change The Way You Think* (Thought Catalog, 2021) at 59.
3. Kenneth Cloke and Joan Goldsmith, "In mediation as in life, truth is relative" (2001) *Dispute Resolution Journal* 56(2) at 86 <http://libproxy.smu.edu.sg/login?url=https://www.proquest.com/scholarly-journals/mediation-as-life-truth-is-relative/docview/198086977/se-2?accountid=28662> (accessed 5 April 2022).
4. Daniel Pollack and Elisa Reiter, "'I'm right.' 'No, I'm right.' New techniques for medicating high-conflict disputes." *Texas Lawyer* at 4 (22 June 2021) <https://www.researchgate.net/publication/352666721_'I'm_right'_'No_I'm_right'_New_techniques_for_mediating_high-conflict_disputes> (accessed 5 April 2022).
5. Subordinate Courts, Singapore and Butterworths Asia, *Families in conflict: theories and approaches in mediation and counselling* (Butterworths Asia, 2000) at 33.
6. Jessica Katz Jameson, Andrea M Bodtker and Tricia S Jones, "Like talking to a brick wall: Implications of emotion metaphors for mediation practice" (2006) *Negotiation Journal* 22(2) 199–207.
7. Beth E Maultsby and Kathryn Flowers Samler, "High conflict family law matters and personality disorders" (2013) at 2 <http://www.mediationworx.co.za/media/attachments/2017/11/01/high-conflict-matters-and-personality-disorders.pdf> (accessed 5 April 2022).
8. Ibid at 1.
9. Joan B. Kelly, "Mediation and psychotherapy: Distinguishing the differences" (1983) *Mediation Quarterly* at 39 <https://doi.org/10.1002/crq.39019830105> (accessed 5 April 2022).
10. Ibid at 34.
11. Id.
12. Ibid at 36.

13. Ibid at 40.
14. Ibid at 35.
15. Joan Jutta Lachkar, "Beware of High Conflict Personality Disorders: Implications for Mediation" (2022) *International Journal of Clinical and Experimental Medicine Research* 6(1) at 84 <http://www.hillpublisher.com/UpFile/202201/20220119172749.pdf> (accessed 5 April 2022).
16. Id.
17. *Kelly*, see note 9 at 44.
18. Ibid at 33.
19. *Maultby and Samler*, see note 7 at 1.
20. *Lachkar*, see note 15 at 85.
21. Bill Eddy, *High conflict people in legal disputes* (Unhooked Books, 2012) at 29.
22. *Maultby and Samler*, see note 7 at 3.
23. *Lachkar*, see note 15 at p 85.
24. Daniel Bowling and David Hoffman, "Bringing peace into the room: The personal qualities of the mediator and their impact on the mediation" (2000) *Negotiation Journal* 16(1) at 11.
25. *Pollack and Reiter*, see note 4 at 6.
26. Connie JA Beck and Bruce D Sales, *Family mediation: Facts, myths, and future prospects* (American Psychological Association, 2001) at 41.
27. David A Hoffman, "Paradoxes of Mediation" (2002) *Dispute Resolution Magazine* 9(23) at 30.
28. Richard Gillespie, *Manufacturing Knowledge: A History of the Hawthorne Experiments* (New York: Cambridge University Press, 1991) at 3.
29. *Bowling and Hoffman*, see note 24 at 10.
30. Fritjof Capra, *The Web of Life* (New York: Anchor Books, 1996).
31. *Bowling and Hoffman*, see note 24 at 11.
32. *Subordinate Courts, Singapore and Butterworths Asia*, see note 5 at 35.
33. Susie Sweeper and Kim Halford, "Assessing adult adjustment to relationship separation: The Psychological Adjustment to Separation Test (PAST)" (2006) *Journal of Family Psychology* 22 at 633.
34. Bill Eddy, *It's All Your Fault!: 12 Tips for Managing People who Blame Others for Everything* (Unhooked Books, 2012) at 201.
35. Renee Gendron, "The Meanings of Silence During Conflict" (2011) *Journal of Conflictology* 1(7) at 2.
36. Hilary Astor, *Mediation and Violence Against Women. National Committee on Violence Against Women* (ACT: CPN Publications, 1991).

37. Bruce Turner and Robin Saunders, "Mediating A Planning Scheme Amendment: A Case Study in the Co-Mediation of a Multi-Party Planning Dispute" (1995) *Australian Dispute Resolution Journal* 6.
38. Alison Taylor, "Concepts of neutrality in family mediation: Contexts, ethics, influence, and transformative process" (1997) *Mediation Quarterly* 14(3) at 220.
39. Sarah C Grebe, "Ethics and the Professional Family Mediator" (1992) *Mediation Quarterly* 10(2) at 161.
40. Claire Baylis and Robyn Carroll, "Power Issues in Mediation" (2005) *Alternative Dispute Resolution Bulletin* 7(8) at 5.
41. John R P French and Bertram Raven, "The Bases of Social Power" in Dorwin Cartwright (ed.) *Studies in Social Power, University of Michigan Institute of Social Research* (Ann Arbor, 1959) at 256.
42. Amanda Ripley, *High Conflict: Why We Get Trapped and How We Get Out* (Simon and Schuster, 2022) at 198.
43. James Wall and Rhonda Roberts Callister, "*Ho'oponopono: Some Lessons from Hawaiian mediation*" (1995) *Negotiation Journal* 11(1) at 50.
44. *Lachkar,* see note 15 at 85.
45. Jerome Front., "A Quiet Revolution" (2008) *Psychotherapy Networker* 32(1).
46. Gregory Bateson, *Steps to An Ecology of Mind.* (New York: Ballantine, 1972). See also Gregory Bateson, *Mind and Nature: A Necessity Unity.* (New York: Dutton, 1979).
47. Howard H Irving and Michael Benjamin, *Therapeutic family mediation: Helping families resolve conflict* (Sage, 2002) at 8.
48. Tony Whatling, *Mediation skills and strategies: A practical guide* (Jessica Kingsley Publishers, 2012) at 73.
49. *Gendron,* see note 35 at 4.
50. *Maultby and Samler,* see note 21 at 24.
51. Ibid at 26.
52. *Eddy,* see note 7 at 1.

Chapter 6 The Fundamental Concept of Voluntariness in Mediation: Is Mandatory Mediation an Oxymoron?

1. Rules of Court 2021 (Cap. 322).
2. Frank E.A. Sander, H. William Allen and Debra Hensler, "Judicial (Mis)Use of ADR — A Debate" (1996) *University of Toledo Law Review* 27(4) 885–886.

3. Women's Charter 1961, Section 50(3A).
4. Dorcas Quek, "Mandatory Mediation: An Oxymoron? Examining the Feasibility of Implementing a Court-Mandated Mediation Program" (2010) *Cardozo Journal of Conflict Resolution* 11(2) 488.
5. See Form 6A, State Courts Practice Directions.
6. See the State Courts Practice Directions and the Supreme Court Practice Directions.
7. Mediation Act 2017, Section 3(1)(D).
8. *Sander, Allen and Hensler,* see note 2.
9. *Quek*, see note 4.
10. Rules of Court 2021, Order 5, Rules 2(3) and 3(4).
11. David Winston, "Participation Standards in Mandatory Mediation Statutes: "You Can Lead A Horse to Water...." (1996) *Ohio State Journal on Dispute Resolution* 11(1) 193.
12. Stella Vettori, "Mandatory Mediation: An Obstacle to Access to Justice" (2015) *African Human Rights Law Journal* 15(2) 359.
13. Ibid at 361.
14. Rules of Court 2021, Order 21, Rule 4(c).
15. Rules of Court 2021, Order 5, Rules 1(2) and 1(4).
16. Ronan Feehily, "Creeping Compulsion to Mediate, the Constitution and the Convention" (2018) *Northern Ireland Legal Quarterly* 69(2) 132.
17. *Vettori*, see note 12.
18. Rules of Court 2021, Order 9, Rule 6(1).
19. Chief Justice Sundaresh Menon, "Mediation and the Rule of Law", Singapore Mediation International Mediation Centre Keynote Address (2017) <https://simc.com.sg/blog/2017/03/23/mediation-rule-law/>.
20. *Quek,* see note 4.
21. Women's Charter 1961, Section 50(3A), read with Women's Charter (Mediation and Counselling) (Prescribed Persons) Rules 2011 Section 2(1)(c).
22. Women's Charter 1961, Section 50(3B).
23. Family Justice Courts Practice Directions, Part V at [12].
24. Eunice Chua, "Mediation in the Singapore Family Justice Courts: Examining the mandatory mediation model under the judge-led approach" (2019) *Civil Justice Quarterly* 38 104.
25. Timothy Hedeen, "Coercion and Self-determination in Court-Connected Mediation: All Mediations Are Voluntary, But Some Are More Voluntary than Others" (2005) *Justice System Journal* 26(3) 278.

26. Rules of Court 2021, Order 3 Rule 2(3).
27. *Sander, Allen and Hensler,* see note 2.
28. *Quek,* see note 4.
29. Paul Randolph, "Compulsory mediation? Paul Randolph asks why litigation is so often preferred to mediation" (2010) *New Law Journal* 499.
30. Melissa Hanks, "Forum: Perspectives on Mandatory Mediation" (2012) *The University of New South Wales Law Journal* 951.
31. *Quek,* see note 4.
32. *Hanks,* see note 30.
33. Civil Justice Council, UK "Mandatory (alternative) dispute resolution is lawful and should be encouraged" (2021) <https://www.judiciary.uk/announcements/mandatory-alternative-dispute-resolution-is-lawful-and-should-be-encouraged/>. The report is available at <https://www.judiciary.uk/wp-content/uploads/2021/07/Civil-Justice-Council-Compulsory-ADR-report-1.pdf>.
34. *Halsey v Milton Keynes* [2004] 1 WLR 3002.
35. David Parratt and Rebecca Farrell, "To order or not to order compulsory ADR: there is no question" (2021) 3PB Barristers at [3].
36. Ibid at [9].
37. Ibid at [3].
38. *Quek*, see note 4.
39. *Parratt and Farrell*, see note 35.
40. *Quek*, see note 4.
41. Chief Justice Sundaresh Menon, "The Common Law Litigation Process: Time For a Rethink?", Australian Academy of Law Patron's Address (23 October 2014) <https://www.academyoflaw.org.au/resources/Publications/Menon_The%20Common%20Law%20Litigation%20Process%20-%20Time%20for%20a%20Rethink%20on%20.pdf>.
42. Ibid at 36.
43. Ibid at 33.
44. *Menon* (2017), see note 19.
45. Paul Randolph, "Compulsory mediation? Paul Randolph asks why litigation is so often preferred to mediation" (2010) *New Law Journal* 500.
46. See Amendments to Supreme Court Practice Directions, Part IIIA: Alternative Dispute Resolution, Appendix I — Guidelines for advocates and solicitors advising clients about ADR at 3[.5].
47. *Hanks*, see note 30.

48. *Menon* (2014), see note 41 at [36].
49. *Hanks*, see note 30.
50. *Menon* (2017), see note 19.
51. Simmons & Simmons, "Mandatory Mediation? "Alternative" dispute resolution no longer" (2021) <https://www.simmons-simmons.com/en/publications/ckqv222ah1dhb0903c56f9u0b/mandatory-mediation-alternative-dispute-resolution-no-longer>.
52. *Quek*, see note 4.
53. Chief Justice Sundaresh Menon, "Setting the Stage for Mediation's Golden Age", India-Singapore Mediation Summit Address (17 July 2021) at [4] <https://www.judiciary.gov.sg/docs/default-source/news-docs/india-singapore-mediation-summit---'setting-the-stage-for-mediation's-golden-age'-(final2).pdf?sfvrsn=79164268_0>.
54. *Hedeen*, see note 25.
55. Jacqueline Nolan-Haley, "Mediation Exceptionality" (2009) *Fordham Law Review* 78(3) 1251.
56. Tham Yuen-C, "Budget debate: Mandatory mediation being considered for some community disputes" *The Straits Times* (10 March 2022) <https://www.straitstimes.com/singapore/politics/budget-debate-mandatory-mediation-being-considered-for-some-community-disputes>.
57. *Menon* (2014), see note 41 at [33].
58. Andrew Phang, "Mediation and the Courts — the Singapore Experience", 4th Asian Mediation Association Conference Address (2016) at [4].
59. Ibid.
60. *Menon* (2021), see note 53.

Chapter 7 In Pursuit of Therapeutic Justice: Mediation and Singapore's Family Justice System

1. SG Courts website, "Therapeutic Justice in the Family Courts" <https://www.judiciary.gov.sg/who-we-are/therapeutic-justice>.
2. Ibid.
3. Leong Wai Kum, "Custody and Guardianship" in *Elements of Family Law in Singapore*, (LexisNexis, 3rd Edition, 2018) 293–342 at [9.126]. See also [9.127]–[9.132].
4. *SG Courts website, "Therapeutic Justice in the Family Courts"*, see note 1 at "FAQ 3. How is therapeutic justice applied for family cases?".

5. *SG Courts website, "Therapeutic Justice in the Family Courts"*, see note 1 at "FAQ 5. What is the therapeutic justice approach and why did the FJC decide to adopt therapeutic justice for family cases?".
6. Sim Khadijah Binte Mohammed, "Mediation Advocacy" in *Legal Skills: A Complete Guide* (Sweet & Maxwell, 2019) 345–369 at [7.2.1] and [7.2.2].
7. Ibid. See also Singapore Mediation Centre's Overview of Services, <https://www.mediation.com.sg/our-services/overview-of-services/mediation/> under "What is mediation?".
8. I am referring to the confidentiality in the process. See also SMC's website, note 7, at "Benefits of mediation" and *Khadijah,* note 6, at [7.2.9] and [7.2.10].
9. *SMC website,* see note 7 at "Benefits of mediation".
10. *Khadijah,* see note 6 at [7.2.16].
11. Mediation being in alignment with the "less-adversarial, child-centred" model of family justice system; see Singapore International Mediation Institute, "Women in Mediation: An Interview with The Honourable Justice Debbie Ong" (2018) at Q1 <https://www.simi.org.sg/Resources/Feature/IWHM/2018/DebbieOng>.
12. SG Courts website, "Mediation at the Family Dispute Resolution Division" at "The family dispute resolution process for cases with young children" <https://www.judiciary.gov.sg/family/mediation-at-family-dispute-resolution-division>.
13. Ibid at "Mediation in the Family Justice Courts".

Chapter 8 Children Should Be Heard To Be Seen: Including Children in Divorce Mediation

1. *CX v CY (minor: custody and access)* [2005] 3 SLR(R) 690 at [26].
2. *VJM v VJL and another* [2021] SGHCF 16.
3. Ibid at [17].
4. Debbie Ong, "Parents and Custody Orders — A New Approach" (1999) *Singapore Journal of Legal Studies* 205–228 at 233 <http://www.jstor.org/stable/24867784>.
5. Ibid.
6. *TAU v TAT* [2018] 5 SLR 1089.
7. Ibid at [12].
8. Ibid.
9. Janet Smithson *et al.*, "The 'child's best interests' as an argumentative resource in family mediation sessions" (2015) *Discourse Studies* 17(5) at 620 <https://journals.sagepub.com/doi/full/10.1177/1461445615590722>.

10. Ibid.
11. Roger Fisher & William Ury, Getting to Yes: *Negotiating an Agreement Without Giving In* (Boston: Houghton Mifflin, 1991).
12. Bobette Wolski, "The 'new' limitations of Fisher and Ury's model of interest-based negotiation: Not necessarily the ethical alternative" (2012) *James Cook University Law Review* 19 at 141 <http://classic.austlii.edu.au/au/journals/JCULawRw/2012/7.pdf>.
13. *Smithson*, see note 9 at 613.
14. Ibid at 619.
15. Ibid.
16. The United Nation's Convention on the Rights of the Child, 20 November 1989, UNTS 1577, Article 12(1).
17. Ibid.
18. Siau Ming En, "Mediation 'vital as more people turn to courts for family disputes", TODAY (2 October 2015) <https://www.todayonline.com/singapore/mediation-vital-more-people-turn-courts-family-disputes>.
19. Jennifer E McIntosh, Yvonne D Wells & Caroline M Long, "Child-focused and child-inclusive Family Law dispute resolution: One year findings from a prospective study of outcomes" (2007) *Journal of Family Studies* 13(1) at 21 <https://doi.org/10.5172/jfs.327.13.1.8>.
20. Ibid at 22.
21. Ibid at 21.
22. Felicity Bell, Judy Cashmore, Patrick Parkinson and Judi Single, "Outcomes of Child-Inclusive Mediation" (2013) *International Journal of Law, Policy and the Family* 27(1) <https://doi.org/10.1093/lawfam/ebs017>.
23. McIntosh, Wells and Long, see note 19 at 21.
24. Judy Cashmore, "Children's participation in family law matters" in Christine Hallett and Alan Prout (eds.), *Hearing the voices of children: Social policy for a new century* (Routledge, 2003).

Chapter 9 Challenges to Ratification and Practice of the Singapore Convention on Mediation in China

1. See the United Nations Convention on International Trade Law website, <https://uncitral.un.org/en/texts/mediation/conventions/international_settlement_agreements/status>.
2. See Article 10, Opinions of the Supreme People's Court on Establishing a Sound Mechanism for the Resolution of Conflicts and Disputes between Litigation and Non-litigation (Fafa [2009] No. 45) and Article 1, Provisions

of the Supreme People's Court on the Procedures for Judicial Confirmation of People's Settlement Agreements Resulting from Mediation (Fa Shi [2011] No. 5).

3. See, Article 12, Opinions of the Supreme People's Court and the Ministry of Justice on the Pilot Work of Lawyer Mediation (Sifa Tong [2017] No. 105); Article 8, Opinions of the Supreme People's Court and the All-China Federation of Industry and Commerce on Promoting the Construction of a Diversified Dispute Resolution Mechanism in the Private Economy by Taking Advantage of Chamber of Commerce Mediation (Law [2019] No. 11).
4. In China's practice, the judicial authorities consider "agreements reached through mediation by administrative organs, commercial mediation organizations, industrial mediation organizations or other organizations with mediation functions" and "agreements reached through mediation appointed/commissioned by the people's courts" as the subject of judicial confirmation. *See,* Article 20, Opinions of the Supreme People's Court on Establishing a Sound Mechanism for the Resolution of Conflicts and Disputes between Litigation and Non-litigation (Fafa [2009] No. 45); Article 11, Guiding Opinions of the Supreme People's Court on Further Improving the Mechanism for Assigned Mediation (Fafa [2020] No. 1); Article 1, Provisions of the Supreme People's Court on Certain Issues Concerning Civil Mediation in the People's Courts (Fa Shi [2020] No. 20).
5. In 2018, the Ministry of Justice specified that individual mediation offices shall comply with the provisions of China's People's Mediation Law, shall not charge any fees, and the mediation agreement shall be stamped with the seal of the People's Mediation Committee to which it belongs. *See,* Article III (iii) 6, Guidance of the Ministry of Justice on Promoting the Construction of Individual Mediation Offices (Sifa Tong [2018] No. 119).
6. See Chen Shen, "Opportunities, Challenges and Strategies: A Current Overview of Commentaries Towards the Singapore Convention Within China" (2021) *Asian Social Science* 17(12).
7. The U.S. Uniform Mediation Act of 2001 changed the role of the mediator from "conduct" to "facilitate".
8. See Li Hao, "Procuratorial Supervision of Civil Mediation Letters" (2014) *Legal Studies* 3(3) 147.
9. *Chen*, see note 6.
10. In order to avoid major changes in the domestic legal regime of mediation by the parties, the drafting group of the Convention took the pragmatic

decision to limit the scope of application of the Convention to international mediation. In other words, China can relax the scope of application of the Convention to international mediation without changing is domestic mediation system.

11. See Yang Bingxun, "The Singapore Convention on Mediation and the Development of China's Commercial Mediation System" (2020) *Beijing Arbitration* 1120.
12. See Ministry of Commerce press release, "Ministry of Commerce and Other Departments Jointly Release 2019 Annual China Foreign Direct Investment Statistical Bulletin" (16 September 2020) <http://hzs.mofcom.gov.cn/article/date/202009/20200903001523.shtml>.

www.ingramcontent.com/pod-product-compliance
Lightning Source LLC
LaVergne TN
LVHW011816200926
848484LV00005B/1212
9789811285240